I believe at the deepest part of the heart of every leader serving the Lord Jesus is a genuine desire to please God and see His Kingdom flourish. If you have the courage to humbly and daily confront the pride, sin, selfishness, fear of failure, envy, and lies this world assaults every leader with, then hearing "well done my faithful servant" from our Lord is certain. *Set Free to Lead* provides a clear, honest, practical, and biblical path that, when embraced by our souls, will absolutely lead to the abundant life Jesus boldly promises us.

LARRY D. ANDREWS,
Principal, OneAccord

Leadership today is seen as an opportunity to flaunt authority, wield influence and amass power. Upon this backdrop, Scott Rodin calls us to a new brand of steward leadership—leaders who are marked by humility, service, and focused upon God's Kingdom over our kingdom. The message throughout this book challenged me to evaluate the areas in my life where I have been given leadership opportunities—at home, at work, in the church—and live into the stewardship role Jesus calls me to. This book should be a must read for all leaders!

BOBBY ARKILLS,
Executive Director, Tacoma Area Youth for Christ

Dr. Scott Rodin's *Set Free to Lead* is biblical, practical and transformational. Most leadership books start with the question, "What do I need to do to be a good leader?" But in this book, you will learn that "a steward leader is first a faithful steward who is then called to lead." You will also discover The Seven Keys to the Freedom of a Steward Leader. This is a must have resource for every Christian worker.

ADEL AZMY,
NABLA Initiative, Alexandria, Egypt

I am thrilled Scott Rodin's new book, *Set Free To Lead*, brings the biblical principles of steward leadership to everyone in a clear and compelling way. These principles are liberating for anyone, but they are critical guideposts for leaders. Dr Rodin's innovative teaching inspired me to envision a new mindset of leadership and success as the CEO of a medical foundation. Not only was I set free to lead, but all levels of my wonderful team were set free to accomplish more than anyone could imagine. If you are ready for a new journey, this book is for you.

DR. PRESTON CAMPBELL,
Former President and CEO, The Cystic Fibrosis Foundation

The Kingdom of God has place for only one King ...and the job is already taken by Jesus our King. All the rest of us are therefore called to be stewards.

By contrast, the way of many leaders is to exercise control. It doesn't take long for these efforts to become chains that bind. These are the chains that Scott talks about in his book. These chains masquerade as a means to secure our leadership position but end up creating a debilitating bondage that robs us of our freedom to serve as effective stewards. If you want to be an effective steward for Christ, this is a book you need to read and learn from. Welcome to the world of being liberated and free to lead...as a true steward.

DR. RAVI JAYAKARAN,
President and CEO, Medical Ambassadors International

Dr. Scott Rodin gives us a transformational leadership model based on systematic theology that leads to true freedom. *Set Free to Lead* takes the leader on a journey of surrender that will last a lifetime and will impact every area of their life. It is refreshing to see a leadership model that moves us to a steward lifestyle and challenges us from the inside out, rather than being based solely on specific leadership skill development. Through Scott's body of work, leaders of influence will know the joy of being builders of God's kingdom as they become *Set Free to Lead*.

Don Johnson,
CEO, IMPACT Coaching and Consulting
Former Superintendent of Schools, Cascade Christian Schools.

Set Free to Lead is the wonderful culmination of Scott Rodin's last three decades of grappling with and honing what it means to be God's faithful steward. He takes all the complex richness of steward theology and presents it in a fresh, new package that is clear and simple enough for anyone to grasp. With this book, leaders will significantly improve their leadership skills and learn practical guidelines to intentionally steward each of life's fundamental relationships—with God, neighbor, self, and creation. It is a must-read for both leaders and laypersons who not only seek greater effectiveness but simply want to tap into a life of greater fulfillment and joy.

Jon Lewis,
Director, Africa Steward Leadership Initiative

Our long wait is finally over for this popular version of the theology of the steward. Scores of leaders from this side of the world benefited from his earlier scholarly books on the subject. Scott Rodin best articulates what it means to live life in its fullness as a steward set free from the bondage of ownership and control. This is what every Christian leader needs to read in order to release the chains that bind us and to find true freedom and joy in the one Kingdom of God.

Dr. Zenet Maramara,
President, Christian Stewardship Association Philippines

Once again, Dr. Rodin has crafted a book which will be both an encouragement and guide to leaders of Christian organizations. Leadership reflecting lives surrendered to God is in greater need than ever in today's often puzzling and seemingly fragmented world. Understanding and embracing the biblical framework of steward leadership shared in *Set Free to Lead* can be a catalyst for your organization and your mission in serving the King of Kings.

JULIE OLSON,
Administrator, Firm Foundation Christian School

We need nourishing books on leadership we can turn to repeatedly as meta-guides throughout our careers rather than quickly-discarded sugar bombs that tell us what to do. Scott Rodin gives us a book to dog-ear, underline, journal about, and take along as a personal, tattered copy to rely on. Rodin distills a lifetime of study and reflection that develops the person who develops the organization that others will lead. One word captures it. Steward.

MARK L. VINCENT,
Founder, Design Group International
and Society for Process Consulting

The highest form of leadership comes with the word STEWARD preceding it. Steward Leadership is a difficult thought for us to grasp because it is so counterintuitive, like nearly all of Christ's principles for living an abundant life. In *Set Free to Lead*, Dr. Rodin has unveiled for us a path to discovering, understanding and developing the Steward Leaders' way and achieving the abundant life that God desires for us. I would invite you to take this path to abundance, and in so doing, discover a deeper, more intimate relationship with God, yourself, those around you and the environment in which you live. You'll find a place of great joy and peace.

HARRIS WHEELER,
Convene Chair

SET FREE TO
LEAD

*Your Guide to Discovering the
Abundant Life of a Steward Leader*

R. SCOTT RODIN

 KINGDOM LIFE PUBLISHING

ISBN: 978-1-7362697-1-8

Contents

Introduction

⊷⊷⊷

BONDAGE VERSUS FREEDOM

Too often, well-intentioned leaders become bound in chains because they accept a way of leading that is not God's way. This bondage can spiral downward with disastrous consequences if truth does not set them free.

This is a book about freedom. Jesus taught us that he came to set us free. Listen to his exchange with the Pharisees from John 8:

> To the Jews who had believed him, Jesus said, "If you hold to my teaching, you are really my disciples. Then you will know the truth, and the truth will set you free." They answered him, "We are Abraham's descendants and have never been slaves of anyone. How can you say that we shall be set free?" Jesus replied, "Very truly I tell you, everyone who sins is a slave to sin. Now a slave has no permanent place in the family, but a son belongs to it forever. So, if the Son sets you free, you will be free indeed. (John 8:31–36)

1

The Apostle Paul reminds us that:

It is for freedom that Christ has set us free. Stand firm, then, and do not let yourselves be burdened again by a yoke of slavery. (Galatians 5:1)

As leaders, we may not see the relationship between leadership effectiveness and freedom in Christ. Yet they are integrally linked. In fact, I believe the single greatest reason that Christian leaders are either ineffective, burned out, or failing is due to their lack of freedom.

Put another way, it is the enemy's goal and desire to put us in bondage. He delights when we wear the heavy chains of stress, anxiety, fear of failure, doubt, discouragement, and despair. In our private life, these chains rob us of the full life God created us to live. For leaders, these chains can destroy us and our institutions if they remain in place. If you have ever felt the heavy burden of these chains as a leader, you know their power.

In Part 1, we will look carefully at both the freedom God offers us and the chains we wear. These three chapters set the stage for your journey of becoming a steward leader. I will define steward leader more thoroughly in the next chapter, but to start, a steward leader is *a faithful steward who has been set free to lead.* Becoming a steward leader is a journey from bondage to freedom that will equip you to lead with freedom and peace and to live the abundant life Jesus promised for every one of us. Thousands of Christian leaders around the world are discovering this freedom for their lives and leadership. As one African leader exclaimed, "This changes everything!"

Welcome to the journey.

Part 1

PREPARING
FOR THE JOURNEY

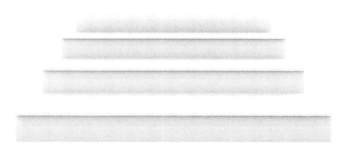

Five Leadership Lessons

───❦───

The journey of the steward leader begins at an intensely personal level. For that reason, I want to start by sharing some personal reflections on my own journey and what I have learned along the way.[1] This includes a very personal confession.

Over my nearly forty years in not-for-profit management and consulting, I have held a number of leadership positions, including seminary president, association president, and company president. I have also held important leadership positions, such as father, husband, and church member.

As I reflect back on these positions through the lens of the steward leader, I have a confession to make. In my roles as a leader, too often I have been wrong. Now, I've not been wrong about everything. In fact, I believe I have been relatively successful in a lot of things I attempted and accomplished in these roles. I could make the usual list of "legacy" items that we leaders do in justifying our time in leading others. There is much to be thankful for, many moments to treasure, and certainly a legacy that I trust will make a difference to generations that follow.

Yet at the very heart of my reflection on my leadership lies this one major conclusion: I've often been wrong in my understanding and preconceived notions of leadership in Christian ministry and in my expectations of others and myself.

---

1 This chapter is adapted from an article that was first published in *The Journal of Leadership Studies*, 2002.

I look back and wonder why this was so. My career path had certainly prepared me for leadership: years of fundraising experience, a PhD from a leading school in Great Britain, successful work in not-for-profit administration, and a knack for strategic planning and vision-casting. I had good experience in managing effective teams and working with not-for-profit boards. There was no lack of preparation for the task. On the personal side, I was brought up in a relatively functional home with wonderful parents and a good relationship with my siblings. Little in my life seems to have been an obstacle to my role as an effective leader at work or at home.

Nor was there a lack of motivation. I have long believed that God has gifted me for leadership. I rose naturally and quickly into key leadership positions wherever I went. It felt right, seemed natural, and was usually satisfying and challenging. So it has been logical to take leadership roles as they came along.

My problem has not been with lack of preparation or motivation, or even with a sense of true calling and a sincere desire to serve God with the best of my skills and abilities. The problem lay solely with my predetermined understanding of what Christian leadership was really all about.

In the early years of my life as a leader, if you had asked me for a scripture that epitomized the leadership ideal, I would likely have pointed you to Nathan's directive to King David: "Whatever you have in mind, go ahead and do it, for the Lord is with you" (2 Samuel 7:3).[2]

I could identify with David as "God's man at God's time," and I believed that God would pour out his wisdom and favor if I could be such a man. After all, there were kingdoms to conquer

---

[2] Unless otherwise noted, all biblical quotations are from the New International Version (Grand Rapids: Zondervan, 2005).

and people to be led. There were great things to be done for the Lord, and no vision was too limited, nor goal too small.

Now, reflecting back on my own leadership experiences and the leadership I have witnessed in my years of consulting work, I would point to a different verse. In speaking of Jesus's incarnation, Paul tells us that Jesus "made himself of no reputation, and took upon him the form of a servant" (Philippians 2:7).[3] The King James's use of the term "no reputation" is especially powerful here. It does not say that Jesus became a man of *bad* reputation, or *questionable* reputation, but simply of *no* reputation. That means reputation, image, prestige, prominence, power, and other trappings of leadership were not only devalued, but they were also purposefully dismissed. Jesus *became* such a man. Not by default or accident, but by intention and design. And it was only in this form that he could serve, love, give, teach, and yes, lead.

In reflecting on my years in the president's office, the church, and the living room, I have come to the conviction that true Christian leadership is an ongoing, disciplined practice of becoming a person of no reputation, and thus, becoming more like Christ in this unique way. In his reflections on Christian leadership, Henri Nouwen refers to this way as resisting the temptation to be relevant. He says,

> I am deeply convinced that the Christian leader of the future is called to be completely irrelevant and to stand in this world with nothing to offer but his or her own vulnerable self.[4]

---

3 Authorized King James Version (Grand Rapids: Zondervan).
4 Henri Nouwen, *In the Name of Jesus* (Crossroads: New York, 1996), 17.

In the past, I have rejected this idea outright. In doing so, I was wrong. Today I see and affirm that this way of leading without respect to reputation lies at the heart of faithful, God-honoring leadership. My journey from the one verse to the other marks a significant progression for me. The former verse was a direct word spoken from God to a specific person, and I extrapolated it to apply to me and to Christian leadership in general. The latter verse was a description of the nature of Jesus to whom I am called to follow simply and humbly. The former focused on God's blessing on my work, the latter on my response of obedience and submission to his nature.

This study of the steward leader has grown out of a combination of my work in holistic stewardship, my study of leadership, and these honest reflections on my own journey. Taken together, I am learning that a steward leader is a faithful steward first. Everything flows from the transformed heart of a faithful steward. As a faithful steward, we do, indeed, offer only our vulnerable self, but we do so with confidence and great joy. That is a new journey from the one I began nearly four decades ago.

I want to comment on five areas where I am learning what it means to be this sort of steward leader. In each area, I have had to confess to my own misunderstanding of what Christian leadership was really all about. In each area, I've started again and embarked on a new journey of transformation that leads to freedom and the joyous obedience of a steward leader.

Anointed versus Appointed

I know of few Christian leaders today who were anointed before they were appointed. We have mostly employed the business model of doing careful searches looking for Christian leaders whom we can appoint to office. We check their credentials, put them through rigorous interviews, and even give them psychological tests before we make the critical appointment. Once in place, we then ask God to bless their work.

The biblical evidence seems to indicate that God selects leaders in the opposite order. Samuel anointed David before appointing him king. The selection criterion for leadership was not based on who would most likely get the appointment, but on whom God had anointed for this task. And appointment without anointment always led to disaster.

I have never been asked in an interview if I sensed God's anointing for this position. I don't know what I would have answered, but the issues and criteria to consider in forming an answer to this question were ones that I never considered in my response to my various appointments.

The reason that anointing is so critical to the task of Christian leadership lies in its nature as the most unique form of leadership on earth. Christian leadership, which we will define as the work of the steward leader, requires nothing less than a complete, wholesale sellout of your life in service to God and God only. It is "losing your life" to the work that God wills to work in you to benefit your institution, school, church, or organization. And the stakes are high. Nowhere else in the Christian life will the price for divided loyalties be so costly for so many for so long. Ineffective and fallen leaders compromise kingdom work, and the effects are both temporal and eternal.

Therefore, Christian leadership is a field that must be entered with the utmost seriousness, and only when one has clearly been anointed for the task. I admit it is difficult to create a set of criteria to guide a search process or to apply to our decisions to determine one's anointing. However, because this is a biblical model, it needs to be explored more deeply in our selection of leaders. So here are two considerations.

On the personal side, perhaps anointing can be discerned in part from a sense of humility that acknowledges that the task to which we are being recruited is beyond even our best skills and abilities. When I think of Joseph, Moses, Esther, David, Ezekiel, and others, their initial response to their call was this admission of their own inadequacies for the job. The result was a complete trust and dependence on God's power, presence, and provision. In short, his anointing.

On the search side, I wonder if we could craft our questions to determine to what extent a candidate sees their dependence on God's power, presence, and provision as the basis for their success in the position. We like it when candidates present themselves as confident, qualified, and competent to do the job well. Are we willing to prioritize this admission of utter dependence as a critical factor in our hiring decisions? If not, might we miss someone whom God may have anointed for a position in favor of someone who looks more qualified in our own eyes?

These are difficult issues, but I pray we begin to struggle with them because we know that with God's anointing comes what every leader seeks: God's power and presence. There is a special blessing bestowed on God's anointed. It is the blessing of God's power manifested in ways only seen through the work of God's chosen. Those whom God has anointed shout, and walls fall. They lift their feeble staff, and seas part. They speak God's word boldly, and movements are begun that free the souls of the oppressed. God's anointed do the miraculous because they are servants of the Almighty. There is a unique presence of God in the lives of those God anoints and calls to leadership through that anointing. Without it, we are continually thrown back upon ourselves to make things work. With it, we have the resources of heaven at our disposal if we will be faithful servants.

For this reason, anointed leaders are sublimely unique people. As God's anointed, they will do anything God asks—*anything.* They will seek God's will with passion. They will not move without it, and they will not be diverted from their course once they have it. God's anointed will love what God loves and hate what God hates. That means loving God's people, God's church, God's environment, God's resources, and God's plan. It also means hating sin in every form and coming against anything that stands between God's loving plan and its accomplishment. God's anointed are people of keen discernment. They are branches who are solidly engrafted into the true vine. God's anointed are servants first, last, and always. And God's anointed have only one passion: to know and do God's will that he might have the glory. In this way, God's anointed are people of no reputation.

I did not come into my leadership positions with a clear sense of anointing as a leader, but I have come to better understand and value the distinction between appointment and anointment. I believe that God's anointing can rest on steward leaders who submit everything to him. God works through leaders who trust him beyond question and rely on him for the totality of their life and work. Anointing begets surrender, and, as we will see later, surrender is the disposition of the heart of the steward leader.

Fighting the Need to Increase

When John the Baptist saw Jesus walking in his presence, he made the declaration, "He must increase, but I must decrease" (John 3:30). Most Christian leaders would say that in their hearts they would wish that Jesus would increase, and they would decrease. But it's hard to decrease in a leadership position. There are natural trappings that distinguish those in leadership, such as salary, title, prestige, priority, power, influence, honor, and advancement. And in each area, there are tempting opportunities for increase. There are also pressures to increase and motivations to build a kingdom in which we house our growing collection of leadership trappings. This desire for the fame and fortune of leadership must be met not only by resistance, but, according to John Adams, we must have "a habitual contempt of them."[5]

Nouwen is even more direct:

> The way of the Christian leader is not the way of upward mobility in which our world has invested so much, but the way of downward mobility ending on the cross… Here we touch the most important quality of Christian leadership in the future. It is not a leadership of power and control, but a leadership of powerlessness and humility in which the suffering servant of God, Jesus Christ, is made manifest.[6]

Perhaps the hardest place to decrease is in the influence and the power we hold over people and decisions. For this reason, we find Christian leaders who are overly directive at best and autocratic at worst. And as a result, we produce churches and ministries that are rife with "learned helplessness." By overestimating our own worth, we help our people depend on us for everything. And that dependence feeds into our need to be needed, to be the "idea person" and visionary, and to be in control. We tell ourselves that the more we lead in this way, the more our leadership is valued and our presence desired.

---

5   John Adams, in David McCullough's *John Adams* (Simon and Schuster: New York, 2001), 19.

6   Nouwen, 62–63.

While serving in my role as seminary president, I remember all too well one situation where I brought a bold idea to the faculty and worked hard to secure their support. It worked. The faculty embraced it, and when it was implemented, it had a significant positive impact on the school and our students. In a very public setting, the achievement was being presented, and when it came time to give credit for it, my name was never mentioned. Have you been in a similar situation? This is the moment when you know whether you are free to be a steward leader. I was still on the journey, and it took me time to work through the frustration of not being credited for the idea. Yet in the end, the kingdom of God was served, and people were blessed. Shouldn't that be enough?

I wanted credit for my idea and to let people know I was a great leader because of this great idea. Of course, this is not real leadership, but a counterfeit that contributes to *our* increase and expands *our* kingdom. I'll call this type of leader the "owner-leader." This type of leadership does a terrible disservice to our people, leaving them uninvolved and underdeveloped. It wastes resources and limits our ministry, all under the guise of strong leadership and the use of our God-given talents for "getting things done." Robert Greenleaf reminds us that the difference between a true servant-leader who is servant first and the leader-servant who seeks leadership first, lies in the growth of the people who serve under them. The test question is, "Do those served grow as persons; do they, *while being served*, become healthier, wiser, freer, more autonomous, more likely themselves to become servants?"[7]

Steward leaders are stewards over the people and organizations they serve. They cultivate the people they lead in pursuit

---

7   Robert K. Greenleaf, *The Servant as Leader* (Greenleaf Center: Newton Center, 1970), 7.

of the success of the organization. Integrity in leadership resists the temptation for self-increase. Integrity is the personal attribute of honesty, moral behavior, and a value-centered life. Integrity bears witness externally to all that we are internally. It does not derive from or depend upon what is external to us—upon an external increase. And for that reason, God-honoring integrity begins with our inner life in God. Stephen Covey saw integrity as "the value we place on ourselves."[8] By that, he meant that we first must keep faith with ourselves if we are to be trusted and trustworthy to those around us. We must keep the promises we make to our own value system. We will see that for the steward leader, this means that our self-confidence must be grounded in our faith in Christ and our desire to be like him. Our identity is defined by his indwelling. We seek to be Christ-like in our inner being, confident that "He who began a good work in you will be faithful to complete it" (Philippians 1:6). If Christ is truly living in us, as Paul reminds us, then we can, in turn, live for others in our work with integrity.

As a result, as steward leaders, we will have no need to seek to increase in our positions of power. We will have no desire to build our own kingdoms and advance our own reputations. Our lives are hidden with Christ in God (Colossians 3:3) and therefore, it is no longer we who live, but Christ who lives in us (Galatians 2:20). It is only with this kind of integrity that we can seek to decrease as we look away from ourselves to see the work of Christ increase in and through our work as leaders.

Steward leaders empower their people, give away authority, value and involve others, seek the best in and from their people,

---

8   Stephen R. Covey, *Principle-Centered Leadership* (Fireside: New York, 1990), 61.

and constantly lift others up, push others into the limelight, and reward those they lead. All so that God's will may be done in a more powerful way. They seek no glory for themselves, but find great joy in seeing others prosper. They take no account of their reputation, but desire that Jesus's face be seen in all they do. Max De Pree's famous definition is worth repeating: "The first responsibility of the leader is to define reality. The last is to say thank you. In between the leader is a servant."[9]

I have come to understand that the call of the steward leader is a call to a lifestyle of an *ever-decreasing* thirst for authority, power, and influence, where our quest for reputation is replaced by confidence in the power of God's anointing.

Being and Doing

I am a doer. I have the reputation of going one hundred plus miles an hour, always focused on accomplishing objectives, meeting timelines, and crossing things off my infamous "to-do" lists. I like results over process, action over deliberation, and the tangible over the theoretical. And I like to lead people to accomplish goals and realize vision. What gets in my way are processes, people with "issues," using time inefficiently, and undertaking work that seems irrelevant. I say I am committed to transformation, but it must get done on my schedule and show some real results. Does this sound at all like you?

The problem with this style of leadership is that it denies the truth of the gospel and our creation in the image of God (*imago Dei*). As we will see throughout this book, if we are truly made in the *imago Dei,* then our perception of God will necessarily and significantly influence our own self-understanding. If

---

9   James O'Toole, *Leading Change* (Ballantine Books: New York, 1995), 44.

we view God as a solitary entity, an isolated being known for his power and transcendence, then we will be leaders who reflect those characteristics. We will be lone rangers, seeking power and focusing on *doing*. We will see people as means to an end and value the product over the process. If we see God as a distant and detached monarch, we will lead as monarchs.

However, we are people who believe we were created in the image of a triune God. We believe that the Father, Son, and Holy Spirit are three persons, yet one God. And therefore, we understand that relationship defines us as image bearers of this triune God. We learn that to be God's people, we must focus on who we are as people in relationship. We learn that leadership must be concerned with the whole person, and that God's intent for us is to do the work of the kingdom within and through the community of believers. This is the journey of transformation from which we develop the heart of the steward leader.

A proper understanding of our creation in the *imago Dei* also teaches us that what is most important to God is not *what* we do, but *who* we are. Secular leadership experts are waking to the fact that the key to leadership effectiveness is self-awareness.[10] In Christian terms, this means that the leader, through self-awareness and self-criticism, is the one who is transformed first!

Greenleaf recalls the story of a king who asked Confucius what to do about the large number of thieves. Confucius replied, "If you, sir, were not covetous, although you should reward them to do it, they would not steal." Greenleaf goes on to say,

---

10 Among the many authors who are championing the cause of careful self-awareness are James O'Toole, Stephen Covey, Noel Tichy, John Kotter, Peter Block, Warren Bennis, Max De Pree, and Peter Drucker.

This advice places an enormous burden on those who are favored by the rules, and it established how old is the notion that the servant views any problem in the world as in here, inside himself, and not out there. And if a flaw in the world is to be remedied, to the servant the process of change starts in here, in the servant, and not out there.[11]

Before God can do a great work in an organization, that work must be done first in the heart of the leader. This is what I have learned about being a steward leader. Unless God has taken our hearts captive, all our good "doing" will lack spiritual integrity and Christlike authority. Our work will expose the absence of God's anointing. And it is at the exact moment that we think we "have it all together" that we cease to be usable in the work of the kingdom.

If I could put one Bible verse on the desk of every pastor and every Christian leader in the world, it would be this: "If we say that we have no sin, we deceive ourselves and the truth is not in us" (1 John 1:8). As steward leaders, we must be engaged in a constant process of self-evaluation and repentance. It is so easy for us to be tempted in a variety of directions, and when we stray, we impact our entire ministry. Steward leaders undertake their work with a deep humility and a keen awareness of their own weaknesses and shortcomings. They know themselves well, seek accountability, pray fervently, and watch carefully for red flags and warning signals.

Nouwen challenges us to seek this central and defining characteristic of Christian leadership.

---

11 Greenleaf, 34.

The central question [of the heart of Christian leadership] is, are the leaders of the future truly men and women of God, people with an ardent desire to dwell in God's presence, to listen to God's voice, to look at God's beauty, to touch God's incarnate Word, and to taste fully God's infinite goodness?[12]

For this reason, the greatest tools for an effective steward leader are a mirror and a group of allies and accountability partners who will make sure we are looking into it with clarity and focus.

Becoming a leader of no reputation means not being afraid to stare down your weaknesses and uncover the messy stuff in your private world. It means letting God transform you. And more importantly, it means knowing how much you need that transformation, far more than anyone else in your organization. I have come to understand that the development of self-awareness and personal transformation lies at the heart of the steward leader. And when this ongoing transformation is added to the desire to decrease while Christ increases, all under the anointing power of the Spirit, the steward leader begins to emerge.

Leadership is a Miracle

One of the greatest gifts I received during my term as seminary president came from my colleague Ron Sider in the form of a book entitled *Leadership Prayers* by Richard Kriegbaum. The honesty and humility in these prayers bear witness to the heart of a faithful leader. In his prayer for trust, Kriegbaum offers these words:

I love you, God. You know I do. How natural it is to love you. You are perfect. You are beautiful, pure, powerful,

---

12 Nouwen, 29–30.

absolutely truthful, and kind. You have been so generous to me that just saying thank you seems pitiful sometimes. But far more powerful in my life is knowing and feeling that you love me. You know exactly and completely who I am—all my ugly thoughts, my mangled motivations, my pretending, my irrational fears, my pride, and my unfaithfulness—and you still love me. I know you love me. You know me, and yet, because you love me, you let me lead others. I do not understand it, but I am grateful.[13]

In reading these words back through the lenses of my experience, I have concluded that when God uses any of us to lead effectively, it is nothing short of a miracle. When we place the complex and demanding role of a godly leader next to an honest self-awareness of our own sinfulness and incompetence, we are thrown wholly upon the grace of God and his faithfulness if we are ever to lead anyone anywhere.

I have come to learn that we must approach leadership in dependent humility. As I will say throughout this book, the sole responsibility of the steward leader is joyous, responsive obedience. Throughout history, God looked to the least, the weakest, the outcast, the untalented, the sinful, and the rejected to give great leadership at historic times. I don't think he has changed that approach today. If we are honest as leaders, we know that our capacity to lead is easily exceeded by the size and complexity of our call. We know that there are others more talented, more prepared, more spiritual, and more courageous than are we. But

---

13 Richard Kriegbaum, *Leadership Prayers* (Tyndale House: Wheaton, 1998), 22.

great, godly leaders have always worked at that miraculous inter-section where humility and faith meet the awesome presence and power of God's spirit. And the miracle of leadership happens. It doesn't mean that we don't prepare ourselves, hone our skills, and seek to be the best we can be for the kingdom. What it does mean is that in the end, all that we bring will fall woefully short of what is required, and we will be ever thrown again into the grace and faithfulness of God to work the miracle of leadership in and through us, using our small pile of skills and talents for his glory.

When God uses us to lead, and lead effectively, we should fall on our knees in wonder and thanksgiving that we have seen again this miracle worked in our midst. However, it is far too easy for us to take ownership of this miracle and to believe that these results are due to our own wonderful abilities and leadership qualities. If and when we make this subtle yet devastating shift, we become owner-leaders and the efficacy of our leadership for the kingdom is over. We are on our own, cut off from the power and provision of the Spirit. Every leader finds himself or herself at that place at some point in their work, and it is a terrifying place to be!

Godly leadership is the miracle of God's use of our earthen vessels for the glorious work of his kingdom. To miss this mirac-ulous aspect of leadership will threaten everything we do as leaders, and our office or study will be the loneliest place on earth. I have come to better appreciate the miracle of godly leadership and its connection with self-awareness, the need to decrease, and the power of God's anointing as a defining charac-teristic of the steward leader.

Seeking the Right Applause

A bookmark of mine carries a thought that has stayed with me throughout my years in leadership. It reads, "It doesn't matter if the world knows, or sees or understands, the only applause we are meant to seek is that of nail-scarred hands." Leaders are exposed to opportunities to generate applause. It can come in the form of commendation from the board, approval of our decisions by employees, recognition of our institution's work by constituencies, admiration of our leadership abilities by coworkers, and words of appreciation from our congregation, family, and friends.

As public figures, we receive both the undue criticism for the failures of our institutions and the unmerited praise for their successes. The true calling of leadership requires us to accept the former and deflect the latter. That is, our job is to take the blame for mistakes made by those under our leadership and to deflect the praise by redirecting it to those most responsible for our success. In this way, we keep ourselves in balance, never taking the criticism too personally and not accepting the praise too easily. This balance is difficult to maintain, yet keeping it leads to the joy of finding freedom in leadership—a central concern of this entire book. Steward leaders are *free*! We can know freedom from the tyranny of self-preservation and advancement only as we accept criticism and deflect praise. The success of the steward leader lies significantly in his or her ability to keep this twofold movement of leadership in balance. Leaders who inflict pain lose trust and dishearten their people. Leaders who absorb praise produce resentment and sacrifice motivation.

Two significant temptations come into play here. The first is the fear of rejection that causes us to run from confrontation. The second is the desire to make everyone happy and to measure our performance, our effectiveness, and our "leadership" on that scale. The two are very closely related. The first temptation is motivated by the idea that good leaders will not generate conflict. It is the fear that the rejection of our role as leader is a rejection of our personhood and character. It's generated from that deep-seated desire to hear the applause of all with whom we work.

The second temptation is to lead by reacting. We see which way the wind is blowing and steer that direction, regardless of the situation. We do not want our people to be critical, to question our decisions, or to disagree with our reasoning. We want harmony and unity, which is commendable. But left unchecked, this desire will cause us to sacrifice courage, vision, and risk-taking. It will bring us momentary applause, but will ruin us in the end. To use a variation on a quote from Ralph Waldo Emerson, some leaders worry themselves into nameless graves, while here and there, some forget themselves into immortality.

So we must ask ourselves just what kind of applause we are seeking. If it is human applause that we need to validate, affirm, and encourage us, we will also find that same applause binds us, boxes us in, and ultimately strangles the life out of us. When our daily self-worth and the measure of our effectiveness come primarily from the reaction of those with whom we work, then we are finished as leaders.

Consider how many decisions you are called upon to make in any given day, some in private, some in meetings, and some in the public arena. Every day, there are multiple opportunities to make "applause-generating" decisions. And sometimes, the temptations to make them are enormous, especially when considering the price that would be paid if other alternatives were chosen.

Now consider how often God's will and following his word points you down a different path. I believe this path is the journey of the steward leader. It is at that intersection between doing what God is telling us to do and doing the expedient and popular thing that true leadership takes place. It is there that we know to whom we are looking for our affirmation.

The goal of the steward leader must be to go to bed every night with a clear conscience and a right heart with God. God only asks one thing of steward leaders: that we seek with all our hearts to know his will and respond with obedience and joy.

Before taking on one of my leadership positions, I spent a couple of hours with a man whom I respect for his wisdom and leadership abilities. He gave me encouragement and good advice, and before I left, he told me something that both inspires and haunts me to this day. He said, "Scott, in whatever you do, always strive to be a man that God can trust." I now believe that a man or woman that God can trust is one who seeks only the applause of nail-scarred hands. He or she is also one for whom the cultivation of reputation carries no value.

I did not always have a clear understanding of this need for balance in the life of a Christian leader, but I have now come to see it as an essential component for the steward leader in the kingdom of God.

Becoming a Steward Leader of No Reputation

My years in various leadership positions are a study in transformation. I came into so many of them without a clear set of expectations, values, and ideas about Christian leadership. I wasn't thirsty for power or obsessed with the trappings of leadership, but I also wasn't seeking to be a leader of no reputation, nor was I responding to the call because I was a servant *first*. And I have been on a leadership journey ever since.

I used to reject the notion that good Christian leaders were only those who were brought kicking and screaming into the position. I opposed the idea that anyone who "wanted" to be a president or CEO or superintendent or executive director should be automatically disqualified. I still believe that God prepares people for his work, and that some aspects of this approach are not entirely in keeping with our giftedness. However, the truth in this view is that steward leaders are faithful stewards first, and it is as these God-honoring stewards that they are called to lead. For those who see themselves as leaders first, the temptations to stray in leadership are enormous.

> The long painful history of the Church is the history of people ever and again tempted to choose power over love, control over the cross, being a leader over being led. Those who resisted this temptation to the end and thereby give us hope are the true saints.[14]

At this point in my own steward's journey, I have a dramatically different understanding of the faithful leader—an understanding that continues to be transformed today. In the end, our work as steward leaders is all about lordship. Before it is about vision-casting or risk-taking or motivating others or building teams or communicating or strategic planning or public speaking, it is about lordship. Where Jesus is singularly and absolutely lord of our life, we will seek to be like him and him only. That will be our sole calling. We will be called to our work, and that work will carry God's anointing. We will be called to decrease so that Christ may increase. We will be called to *be* people of God before and as we *do* the work of God. And we will be called to pray and look for the miracle of leadership that God may work in our midst.

---

14 Nouwen, 60.

In these ways, in responding faithfully to this calling and striving after these ideals at the cost of everything else that may tempt us, we become steward leaders. And as we do, we will be transformed into the likeness of Christ, becoming steward leaders.

What Is a Steward Leader?

A Definition

Let's start by defining this important title. Simply put,

> A steward leader is first a faithful steward who is then called to lead.

This may seem to be a simple definition, but there is a lot here we need to unpack. First, this definition implies a movement, and that movement is critical for our journey. Most leadership books start from the question, "What do I need to do to be a good leader?" Their process is to define great leadership, compare it to how we lead, change our behavior to that of great leaders, and like magic, we become such a leader. These leadership books teach traits and techniques, implying that if you just do the things great leaders do, you will be transformed into a great leader. Of course, that seldom happens. The problem is not with the quality of the leadership techniques they teach; it is with the assumption that leadership is mostly about what we do and only partially about who we are. That's where we will depart from the common way of teaching about leadership and take a different route.

The process we will share in this book does not start with your life as a leader, but with your life as a *follower* of Jesus. Our approach is this: we must first be transformed in our understanding of what it means to be faithful in our Christian walk

26

before we look at its implications for the way we lead. That is the movement: from who we are *becoming* as disciples of Jesus to the implications of that transformation when we step into a role of leadership. This is where the steward leader is distinct from servant-leadership. Both are biblical, but too often, we can respond to the command to be a servant-leader with the application of behaviors that make us look like servants. When we ask the question, "How would a servant-leader lead?" we have already missed the mark. Put another way, we can practice the techniques of servant-leadership, but never believe in our hearts that we are truly servants. Without a heart change, servant-leadership becomes just another technique in our toolbox we can use when we think it might work.

In this book, we will resist the temptation to offer you a set of rules or principles or traits to follow. Instead, we will start by first paying attention to our journey of becoming a faithful steward, and then discover what it means to be a steward leader. As we let the Holy Spirit transform our understanding of the life of a faithful steward and as we commit to go deeper with Jesus on that journey, we will be prepared to lead in a more faithful and powerful way than ever before. Jesus first wants faithful stewards, and then he calls those stewards into leadership. When our heart is changed, our work as a leader will also be changed. This change is described as the Seven Keys of the Steward Leader. They are not a formula or prescription for leadership. They are the fruit of a transformed heart as seen through the lens of leadership.

What We're Missing

For followers of Jesus, there may be no more joyful text in all of scripture than John 10:10. These words of Jesus and the rich promise he gives us bring a smile to our faces.

I came that you might have life and have it in all its fullness.

Isn't that the life we long for? The abundant life in Jesus? This is the life of peace and not fear, contentment and not continual want, confidence and not anxiety, joy and not grief, calm and not anger, encouragement and not discouragement, hope and not despair. This is not just wishful thinking; it is actually the life Jesus redeemed us to experience every day.

The question is: Are you experiencing that life? Is this a description of your heart, your attitudes, and your response to the challenges of the world? Would the people around you say that this is the way they see you live your life? For most of us, and perhaps for all of us (if we're honest), we have to confess that this picture of the abundant life doesn't look much like our life at all. Why is that? If this is the life promised to us by Jesus, and we love him and seek to follow him, why aren't we experiencing this life every day? What's the problem here? What are we missing?

Well, the problem can be summed up in one simple phrase. The verse that we quoted is not John 10:10, at least not all of it. We too often love to read this part of the verse, but this is only the second half. John 10:10 *starts* with these sobering words,

The thief comes only to steal and kill and destroy.

Jesus minces no words defining the context in which you and I live. Jesus came to give us life; thieves come to kill. Jesus came that we may know abundance; thieves come to steal. Jesus comes to build up; thieves come to destroy.

This is the tension of the Christian life. We want to follow Jesus with our whole heart. We want to be fully committed to him. We don't want to sin. We want to live holy lives and further the kingdom of God. These are all genuine, sincere desires of the follower of Jesus. However, no matter how hard we may try, we continually face the onslaught of those who want nothing more than our total destruction. Behind these thieves stands the one great thief, the enemy who is the author of all that stands against the abundant life in Christ.

This shouldn't cause us to live in fear, because we know that this enemy has already been overcome. However, in this life, we still feel the effects of his assault against us. We sin when we do not want to, we compromise when we want to be committed, we build our own kingdom instead of building God's, and too often, we look more worldly than holy.

Does this describe your own struggles? Is there a better, more abundant, more joyful, and more faithful life waiting for you than the life Jesus redeemed you to live? I believe that Jesus is calling all of us further on our journey to embrace that life!

My prayer is that this book will help you take that journey, first as a follower of Jesus, and then as a Christian leader. To do so, we must begin by understanding this tension in which we live and lead. This means we must recognize this tension as a spiritual battle. The journey is a movement from the old life to the new life. It is a transformation from the old person to the new person. It is dying and rising, taking off the old and putting on the new. We call it the journey of the faithful steward. It is everything the enemy hates and seeks to destroy in us. Yet greater is he that is in us than he that is in the world (1 John 4:4).

This journey requires us to leave behind our chains and discover this amazing, free, and abundant life in Christ. In this book, I invite you to embrace this journey as a series of seven movements:

1. From owner to steward
2. From two-kingdom bondage to one-kingdom freedom
3. From spiritual stagnancy to deep intimacy with Christ
4. From distortion to a balanced understanding of our identity
5. From seeing people as means to valuing them as ends
6. From complacency in how we use God's resources to nurturing his abundance
7. From apathy to embracing the battle as a steward warrior

The Most Important Question
a Leader Will Ever Ask

———✸———

A few years ago, I was asked to give the commencement address at a west coast Christian university. In my message, I considered what I would have told myself if I could go back in time and sit next to myself at my college graduation. Looking back over my years of work, what would I say? What one piece of advice would I give myself as a bright-eyed and hopeful twenty-two-year-old college graduate? My answer was this: "Be careful how you define success, Scott, because it will drive everything you do."

In my forty-plus years of leadership, consulting, and coaching, I have come to believe this is the single most important question we will ever ask ourselves as leaders. How do you define success? I want you to consider two possible ways you may answer that question and the implications of each for your life and leadership.

Outcomes-Based Success

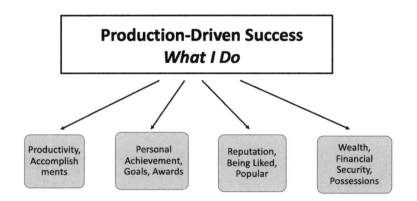

The first way we can measure success is by way of the outcomes of our life and work. We are successful when we have a good job, make a large salary, build a strong marriage, raise kids who are successful, develop a strong retirement account, live in a nice home, go fun places on vacation, build a successful business or ministry, earn the admiration and respect of others, and the list goes on and on. These measurements of success all have to do with what we are able to produce and measure.

When we define success by our accomplishments, we use the metrics of wealth, power, influence, impact, and reputation. This definition of success drives us into a lifelong pursuit of those things the world tells us will determine our value and provide us our happiness and satisfaction. This is success measured by accumulation and achievement. To achieve this definition of success, we must take control, get things done, and believe that our success is up to us. It will drive us to do whatever is needed to attain the success we have defined for our lives. This is success defined in terms of ownership. The more we own, the more we control, the more we have amassed, and the more successful we are.

To make us feel better, we can couch these measurements in

spiritual language. We can serve God by building a large church, having a broad influence for our writing and teaching, and expanding the work of our ministry through more fundraising, more stuff, and more programs. We can claim it is all for the Lord, since it is his work. However, just because we use Christian titles and speak about spiritual outcomes, we still end up using the same metrics of ownership and control. If it is *our* church, *our* ministry, and *our* work, it is still *ours*.

And this brings us to our second point. Our definition of success is what drives us. We invest our lives as leaders in our pursuit of achieving our definition of success. Think about what occupies your time and work. What motivates you to get up and do what you do? What keeps you working late nights and weekends? What causes you stress and anxiety? What drives you each day to do what you do? At the end of it all, you will find your definition of success.

The problem with accomplishments as our means of success is that we never have enough. This is one of the enemy's greatest weapons against Christian leaders. When we shift our definition of success to metrics of ownership and control, the enemy has us on a treadmill that he will use to kill, steal, and destroy the abundant life Christ came to give us. How many Christian leaders do you know who have faced burnout, moral failings, ethical downfalls, and leadership failure? How close have you been to experiencing this yourself? At the center of these stories, you will find this drive, this passion to achieve, constantly pursuing a definition of success that was not in line with God's will and purpose. It may have looked and sounded godly and spiritual, but underneath it was a misplaced understanding of God's definition of success. If you choose human achievement as your definition of success, you can spend your life in an exhaustive pursuit of accomplishing things for God and leave no time or space for him to accomplish his work in you. This is the high cost of charting this course and letting productivity define success.

So what is God's definition of success for us as Christian leaders?

Faithfulness-Based Success

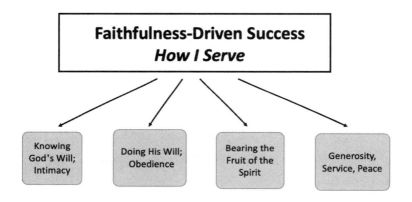

The other choice is to define success by who you are and who you are becoming. As followers of Jesus, we believe that God created and owns everything, including us and our futures. If God is the owner of all life, then our calling is to know the will of the owner and to carry it out with obedience and joy. This is success measured not by the metrics of ownership, but by the life of a faithful steward.

What would it mean to chart a course for your leadership that lifts up faithfulness as your sole definition of success? What would it mean for:

- Your relationship with Christ? Would anything ever be more important than cultivating a more intimate relationship with him?

- Your identity? If you saw yourself as a child of God, would you only need the applause of nail-scarred hands?
- Your relationships? Would the agenda of others become more important to you than your own agenda, and you were set free to serve them?
- Your time and resources? Would you be quick to hear and obey however God wanted you to invest your time and money for the work of his kingdom?

The choice for faithfulness as our driving definition of success is a choice for hope, a choice of promise, a choice of freedom, and a choice of a life of honest engagement, loving our neighbor, lavish generosity, and unapologetic truth.

The Choice

For Christian leaders, choosing faithfulness as our sole definition of success is a choice that sets us free. All other definitions will ultimately put us in bondage. The enemy seizes upon our choice of success as ownership and accomplishment to use it against us and ultimately destroy us. The Holy Spirit awaits our choice of success as faithfulness to set us free from this bondage to live a life of joyful response to the calling of God in every area of our lives.

Leaders who have chosen faithfulness are soft clay in the hands of the Potter who will use them in more powerful ways than they could ever have thought or even imagined. These leaders are driven by one consuming passion—to know God's will and to do it with obedience and joy.

What drives you? How do you define success? Are you leading from the bondage of ownership and control, or from the freedom of faithfulness and joyful obedience?

Part 2

THE SEVEN KEYS

Experiencing the Freedom
of the Steward Leader

———— ⬿⬿⬿ ————

O wner-leaders live in bondage. We have named that bondage with terms such as fear, anxiety, discouragement, envy,
despair, and burnout. These experiences flow from the desire
for control and misplaced identity that lies at the heart of an
owner-leader. I want you now to visualize this bondage as seven
heavy chains. They are wrapped around your shoulders, arms,
waist, and legs. They weigh you down, restrict your movements,
and exhaust your energy. How many of us have tried to live as
effective leaders while shackled in this way?

If this sounds at all like you, the question is: How can you
be set free of them?

Steward leaders are on a journey to just that kind of freedom. It doesn't happen all at once, but slowly, step by step, and
day by day, steward leaders experience the freedom and joy of
a life without chains. They exchange fear for peace, anxiety for
confidence, discouragement for courage, envy for contentment,
despair for hope, and burnout for renewed energy and passion.

This is your invitation to take that journey. In the section
that follows, we will take you on a journey of seven steps, each
one of them offering a key to unlocking the chains that bind you
as a leader. Each step of the journey has four parts: naming what
is at stake, describing the key, showing how it is used, and ending
with prayer and a commitment.

As you apply the keys that unlock these shackles, you will begin to experience more of the free and abundant life Jesus promised. By completing and following your Five Steward Leader Commitments, you have the opportunity to stay on this journey for the rest of your life. As a leader, as a follower of Jesus in every arena in life, this freedom awaits you. Let's start that journey!

Key #1 – It's All God's

Steward leaders *understand that their lives are not their own.* They are stewards of every area of life and resist the temptations to play the role of master. They daily take a posture of listening for God's leading and responding with joyful obedience.

What Is at Stake

We have seen that ownership and control are the weapons the enemy uses to kill, steal, and destroy our lives and our leadership. He knows that full surrender goes against our fallen nature. We want to grasp at control, hold on to power, and push back from vulnerability. The enemy uses our decision to hold back and hold on to put us in bondage. The first heavy chain is the one we wear when we refuse to acknowledge that everything in our life belongs to God—everything. We refuse to give up what we think we possess, believing that by seizing what is ours, we ensure our security and happiness. This is the greatest battle of our leadership, and the battle must be won here if it is to be won in every other area of our life.

Understanding the Key

The key to unlocking the ownership chain starts at the very beginning of each day. When we awake and think about the day that lies ahead—its meetings, challenges, concerns, opportunities, and unknowns—we plan whether we will enter the day as an owner or as a steward. That first, immediate decision will direct our steps the rest of the day. Here is the key to freedom from this first chain. Begin each day with a clear and simple statement, "Lord, it's all yours!"

Our attitude as we start our day will bear witness to our belief that either God owns everything in our life or that we own some of it. It is a one-kingdom versus two-kingdom expression of belief. It is the question whether we will take the heavy chain of ownership and place it back on our shoulders again or to let this be the day we accept God's invitation, unlock the chain, and let it fall. It is a choice we make every day, whether we acknowledge it or not.

How to Use It

We are all on the journey of becoming more faithful stewards. The *first step* is daily stepping off our thrones and surrendering everything back to God, the true owner. Jesus calls to us every day to walk further on this journey. And as we do, we are set free to live the abundant life Jesus promised us. Please take this step! Place everything before God, acknowledging it belongs to him. It starts with a simple prayer before we set foot out of bed.

It's all yours, Lord, it is not mine. It never was. I trust you with my life. Now let me live this day for you, as a faithful steward of all that you have entrusted to me.

One last suggestion. Get yourself a small jar and fill it with dirt. Place it where you see it often, perhaps next to your computer screen or in an office windowsill. Why a jar of dirt? It is there to remind us of this truth. Humanity started as dirt (Genesis 2:7) and dirt is how we will all end (Genesis 3:19). And in between the dirt that is our origin and the dirt that will be our final end, everything in between, *everything* belongs to God. And if that is so, then we are set free to lay off the burden of ownership and live as stewards of what is God's.

It's all his. Let your jar of dirt remind you of that powerful truth every day.

As you think about this journey from bondage to freedom in this first area, let me ask:

- Where are you on that journey?
- Where is God leading you to trust him more?
- Do you live less as an owner and more as a steward each day?
- Have you surrendered everything to God in every area of your life?
- Are you experiencing the freedom and joy of a faithful steward in every area of life?

There is a better, more joyful life that awaits you as a leader. In this new life, there is only one Owner. In this new life, we pray against the need for control and enter a process of letting

God drive from our heart all temptations to play the owner. In this way, we are being freed each day to listen to God's leading and respond with joyful obedience.

Prayer and Commitment

"I will pray each day that God will remind me that everything in my life belongs to him, and I am set free to steward all he has entrusted to me. My first commitment is to daily surrender _____ back to him, and pray for his power to let go and trust him with it."

> I eagerly expect and hope that I will in no way be ashamed, but will have sufficient courage so that now as always Christ will be exalted in my body, whether by life or by death. For to me, to live is Christ and to die is gain. (Philippians 1:20–21)

Key #2 – Developing the Heart of a One-Kingdom Leader

Let's start by defining this term, "one-kingdom leader." To do so, we'll start back in Genesis. If we look at the first two chapters of Genesis, we'll find that we were created for whole relationships that reflect the image of God on four levels: our relationship *with God, with ourself, with our neighbor*, and *with creation*.

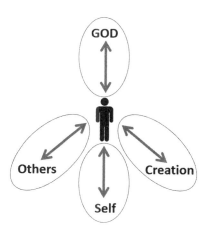

As Adam and Eve lived out those four levels of relationship, they reflected the image of God, and so do we. The meaning of our lives is to be image bearers of our triune God in all four of these relationships. These relationships were given to us as gifts in creation, they were broken in our fall into sin, and they have been restored to us in Jesus Christ. Let's look at these four relationships and what the abundant life looks like in each.

Relationship with God

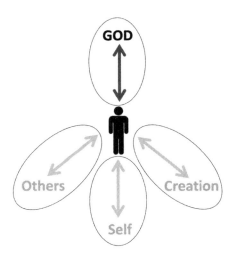

On the first level, our life has meaning when we are at peace and enjoying intimacy with our Savior. Adam and Eve knew this peace and intimacy in the absence of sin. Today, it's in the redemptive work of Jesus Christ that we are restored and reconciled again to God. We can't do it for ourselves. This relationship has been bought for us with the highest possible price, the blood of Christ. God's original intent in creation is now the gift given to us to steward with gratitude and praise.

If we were created for intimate relationship *with God,* then our purpose is to love God with all our heart, soul, strength, and mind. This is our first and highest calling and joy. Worship, Sabbath rest, devotion, prayer, fasting, study, praise, and presence are ways in which we fulfill our purpose in our relationship with God. Intimacy is not something we create; it is the result of total surrender that allows God to do something in us and for us. God draws us near as we submit ourselves to him. And our first and highest response is praise. Abundance at this first level is measured in intimacy and doxology.

Relationship with Ourself

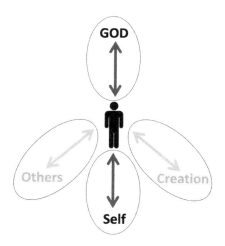

The abundant life on the second level is ours when our identity remains secure in Jesus Christ. We are a child of God. That is the primary and determining source of our self-worth. If we were created for relationship *with ourself*, then our purpose is to have absolute certainty of who we are, why we are here, and what we are to do. This self-understanding was a part of God's loving intent for us when he created humanity in his image.

His purpose for us is found in the balance of our self-perception between the beloved child of God and the sinner saved by grace. It is humility *and* courage. It is the simplicity of the clay vessel *and* the complexity of being the workmanship of God. It is the amazingly powerful place between our recognition that apart from Christ, we can do nothing and in Christ, we can do all things. For Adam and Eve, this was a natural balance before sin and in God's presence, and it produced peace and joy. The abundant life at this level for us is measured by balance in our self-image and the extent of our reliance on God as the sole caretaker of our reputation.

Relationship with Our Neighbor

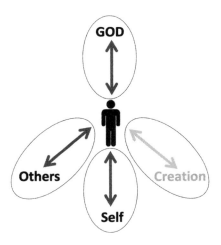

The abundant life on the third level comes from our relationships with others. We were created for relationships. Just as God is triune in his very nature, so we were created to find meaning in our existence in community. If we were created for relationship *with our neighbor*, our purpose is to love our neighbor as we love ourselves. We were created to see our neighbors and their well-being in the same way we see our own, which calls us to value relationships as ends, not means to be used for our own benefit.

The first couple lived in fellowship and community with one another as the natural expression of being image bearers of a tri-une God. The abundant life at this level is measured by the needs of our neighbor, not our own. It is the extent to which we build and value relationships as God's gift and as ends in themselves.

Relationship with Creation

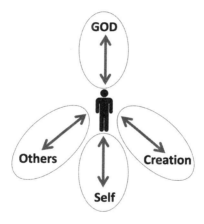

The abundant life on the fourth level is experienced as we live out our status as caretakers of the created world. From Genesis, we see that we were created primarily for this activity. The first task given to God's creation was to tend the garden (Genesis 1:28–30). When we reflect God's caring nurture of us by caring for and nurturing his creation, our lives find real meaning in a world that screams at us that meaning is only found in the hoarding and consumption of resources. Scripture demonstrates for us that we were created to find meaning in the sharing and careful stewardship of God's abundance.

If we were created for a relationship *with creation*, our purpose is to live in harmony with creation: to value it, to tend it, and to take care of it. This includes our time, talents, and resources. All of them! The abundant life at this fourth level is measured by how loosely we hold to our possessions and how closely we heed our call to be caretakers of creation.

Our identity as children of the triune God lies in our lives lived in and through community in holistic relationship, mutually interdependent and seeking the unity of the spirit. That is how we reflect the image of a triune God. This life glorifies God because that is precisely why we were created. It is our purpose. And we fulfill this purpose when we live as we were created to live: in whole, healthy, and productive relationships that reflect the image of God on all four levels. In each, we find the purpose of our lives as God's new creation.

In Eden, there was only one kingdom and one Lord. Everything belonged to the King! The great Reformed theologian and church leader Abraham Kuyper said it best:

> Oh, no single piece of our mental world is to be hermetically sealed off from the rest, and there is not a square inch in the whole domain of our human existence over which Christ, who is Sovereign over all, does not cry: "Mine!"

We were created to be citizens of this one kingdom where Jesus Christ is the one and only Lord. It requires our full surrender to live as stewards of all that is God's. Eden was the perfect, one-kingdom reality that is God's intent for us. However, as we remember from the beginning of John 10:10, there is more to the story.

Lost in Sin

We know that when sin entered into the world, it had a devastating impact on our relationship with God on all four levels.

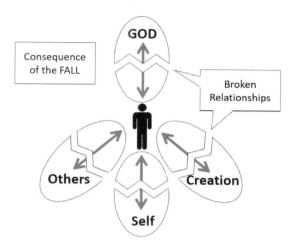

In the fall of Adam and Eve into sin, our ***relationship with God*** was fatally disrupted. The God known in intimacy and fellowship in Eden became the holy and terrible God characterized between Eden and Bethlehem as consuming fire, rushing wind, thunder, earthquakes, and blinding light. The once-intimate relationship between creator and creature was all but destroyed.

We also experienced the loss of ***relationship with ourself.*** Adam and Eve lost their primary purpose in life—tending the garden, loving one another, and fellowshipping freely with God as his beloved creation. Since the fall, the central theme of the history of humanity became our search to find again our purpose and meaning in life. The impact of this loss cannot be overstated. When we lose the guiding sense of purpose for our lives, we are untethered from our moorings and float through life seeking for some other place where we can find security and refuge. Yet every other port disappoints. Every place we look for validation of our own self-worth ultimately fails us, whether that is our occupation, friends, family, wealth, fame, or even our leadership. It is a despairing place to be.

With sin came the rise of *enmity with our neighbor*. Adam blamed Eve; Eve blamed the serpent. The very next story that comes after the fall is of Cain's killing of Abel. Thus begins the human history of "man's inhumanity to man." This inhumanity is a product of the dethroning of God and the coronation of the self as the primary driving force in our lives. This replacement of God with self is the core definition of the impact of sin in our lives and its devastating effects on our relationships with one another.

Finally, in this original sin, we see the rise of conflict in our *relationship with creation*. After the fall, we redefined "dominion" as *domination*, "rule over" became *own and control*, and "subdue" became the justification to *exploit*. It is a postfall understanding of these words that have yielded the grossly mistaken assumption that the earth is ours to use any way we want. The result has been the hoarding of resources for our own use and the ravaging of creation to create those resources.

This is the final scene in this devastating picture of humanity after the fall. Brokenness with God leads to a distorted self-image. This marred image gives rise to the self as the center of life, which in turn uses people and creation in its futile quest for meaning and satisfaction. It is a desperate state, but God did not leave us here!

Restored in Christ

Praise be to God that the restoration Christ accomplished through his own blood was even more holistic than the effect of the fall. Paul tells us that although one transgression brought sin into the world, *how much more* the blood of Christ has covered all sin (Romans 5:9–15). He also proclaims that "as in Adam all men died, even so in Christ have all been made alive" (1 Corinthians 15:22). And we are assured that while sin brought condemnation on the one man, so the blood of Christ brings redemption for all humanity (Romans 5:12–15). In short, *all* that was lost in the fall was *fully and completely* restored in Christ! Just as sin brought brokenness on all four levels, so Christ's redemption brought healing and reconciliation at all four levels.

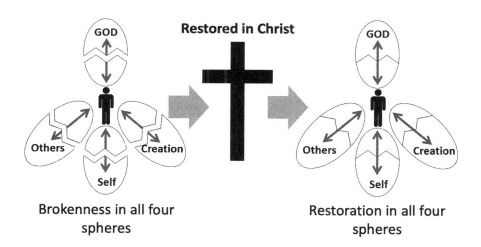

Brokenness in all four spheres

Restoration in all four spheres

Jesus's life demonstrated the right relationship we seek with God, ourself, our neighbor, and our world. Jesus lived the life we could not live. He was obedient where we were disobedient; he was faithful where we were faithless; and he was a neighbor when we passed by on the other side. He knew who he was, why he was here, and what his ministry was to accomplish. He knew his place before God, in the world, and among his people. He did all this while bearing our humanity! He completed in his life and confirmed in his death and resurrection the full requirements of the original relationship between God and humanity. By doing so, Jesus Christ redeemed our relationships at all four levels.

Here is the best news of all. Having redeemed our life in all four levels of relationship, he now gives it back to us *as a gift*. Remember, we lost it through our sin, Christ saved it, Christ redeemed it, and Christ now presents it to us as a gift to be stewarded. We dare not take God's gift—a gift that cost him the blood of his Son—and treat it as if we owned it all along. Instead, we cherish it. This means we see our relationship with our heavenly Father as a gift. We see our self-identity, who we are in Christ, as a gift. We see the people God brings into our lives as a gift. And we see his creation as a valuable gift, including the gifts of time, skills, and resources. They are all his, and we accept them as he gives them to us to steward for him. This is the proper way of understanding God's ownership of everything and our high and holy calling in relationship to all that is God's.

We are now called and equipped to be one-kingdom followers of Jesus, fully surrendered to him in every area of life. Here is what a one-kingdom life looks like.

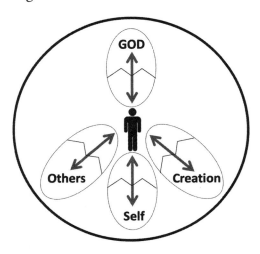

Unfortunately, few of us would claim to be complete, committed, holistic, and one-kingdom people. Despite our desire to be totally and solely committed to Jesus Christ and give everything to him, there are parts of our lives that we hold back from God, and as we do, we build a second kingdom.

Understanding the Key

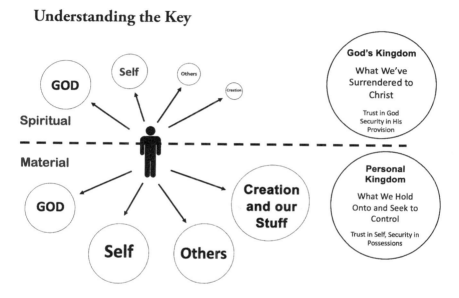

Imagine this picture. You have two kingdoms, each with a wall around it, and in the center is a throne. One kingdom represents our spiritual life. In it, we see our worship, our prayer life, our time studying God's word, and our fellowship with our brothers and sisters in Christ. In this kingdom, Jesus sits on the throne. The second kingdom contains everything we want to hold onto, all the places where we still want to be in control. We may find there our work, our money, our reputation, our health, and our possessions. We may also find some of our relationships there: perhaps our marriage, our kids, and even our friends. As leaders, we may find there our ministry, our church, our business, our donors, our programs, our employees, and so on and so on. Whatever we seek to control, whatever we have held back from God's total sovereign rule, we find in this second kingdom. And in this kingdom, we sit on the throne.

In Genesis 3, Satan tempts Adam and Eve with the promise that if they eat of the forbidden fruit, they will "be like God." Since that moment of trespass, we have become second kingdom builders. In sin, we play the Lord and seek our own control instead of trusting God.

We compromise our citizenship and live as owners of what we cannot own and try to control what is never in our control. This is the battle for lordship, and as leaders, we face this battle every day. Will we live and lead as a steward or an owner? Will we lead from surrender or grasp for control? Will we place our full trust in God or fall back on self-reliance? Will we lead from freedom or continue to be put in bondage?

How to Use It

This book is a call to become a faithful steward and an effective steward leader. We are all on this journey of becoming more faithful stewards. Jesus calls us daily to step off our thrones and surrender everything back to God, the true owner. He calls us to walk further on this journey with him, because he knows that it is on this journey that we are set free to live the abundant life Jesus promised us.

Where are you on that journey? Where is God leading you to trust him more? Do you live less as an owner and more as a steward each day? Have you surrendered everything to God in all four spheres of life? Are you experiencing the freedom and joy of a faithful steward in every area of life?

As you answer these questions and journey further in the

transformation of your spirit from owner to steward, you will be ready to answer this next question: What happens when a faithful steward is called into a position of leadership? Everything you will learn about becoming a steward leader is built on your personal journey of becoming a more faithful steward.

Prayer and Commitment

"I will pray each day that God will give me the wisdom to name the things in my second kingdom, the strength to surrender them back to him, and the freedom to live more fully as a one-kingdom child of God. Today I specifically name the following *one* thing I most need to surrender to him: _____
_____."

Then he said to them all: "Whoever wants to be my disciple must deny themselves and take up their cross daily and follow me. [24] For whoever wants to save their life will lose it, but whoever loses their life for me will save it." (Luke 9:23–24)

Key #3 – Intimacy with Christ Is Our Highest Calling

Steward leaders *seek intimacy with God as their highest calling*. They prioritize activities that nurture this intimacy and reject the temptation to allow urgent matters to rob them of it. They follow God's leading wherever it may take them and the ministry.

What Is at Stake

There is a battle going on for the heart of every Christian leader. Jesus wants our total dependence on him. The enemy wants to sell us the idea that self-reliance is a surer way to happiness and success. The temptation of self-reliance will push us toward the drive to succeed, as we saw in a previous section. From our misplaced definition of success, we will be cut off from the daily desire to know God's will and do it. After all, if we are in charge, if we can rely on our own strength, wisdom, experience, knowledge, and cleverness, we don't need to be led by the Holy Spirit. It's not that we stop believing or trusting or even wanting God to lead us, it's just that we stop *depending* on him. If he shows up and guides us, great. But it is not necessary in order for us to move ahead and lead. God's guidance becomes an option, and we will become impatient waiting too long for it. Instead, we will continually be thrown back upon ourselves to figure out what it means to lead well.

This is a heavy chain that will one day break the back of every leader who throws it over their shoulder and plods ahead in an effort to lead from their own strength. Let me ask, are you working so hard trying to do things for Jesus that you have left him no time to do things in you?

What results from this self-reliance is a stagnancy in our relationship with Christ. Under this chain, prayer and devotion become mechanical and duty driven. Once they stop being the very life force that we depend on as leaders, they will soon become a nicety that we engage in when we have enough time. Once we rely on ourselves to do things for Jesus, we forget the scriptural truth that apart from Christ we can do nothing (John 15:5). This spiritual stagnancy is at the heart of every failing of Christian leaders great or small, whether it be a moral, ethical, or physical failing. That is why we must confront this issue head-on.

Understanding the Key

The key here is simple, yet profound. It is a passionate desire to know the will of the owner and not let anything dissuade us from it. When we acknowledge that God is the owner of everything, what must follow is this passion to know his will, even if it means setting our "doing" aside in order to sit as his feet and listen.

Can you do that? In your leadership role, are you free to value your time being in God's presence as highly as doing God's work? This is a critical question for every Christian leader. Both Mary and Paul knew that this truth was quite extraordinary, even life-changing. Jesus makes the remarkable claim of Mary that she discovered the one thing that is needed (Luke 10:41–42). Martha can't see it. She is distracted by things she considers to be extremely important. They upset her and worry her, causing her to become frantic and irritated. Sound familiar?

Paul, on the other hand, seems to have lost touch with reality in his letter to the Philippians:

> If someone else thinks they have reasons to put confidence in the flesh, I have more: circumcised on the eighth day, of the people of Israel, of the tribe of Benjamin, a Hebrew of Hebrews; in regard to the law, a Pharisee; as for zeal, persecuting the church; as for righteousness based on the law, faultless. But whatever were gains to me I now consider loss for the sake of Christ. What is more, I consider everything a loss because of the surpassing worth of knowing Christ Jesus my Lord, for whose sake I have lost all things. I consider them garbage, that I may gain Christ and be found in him. (Philippians 3:5–9)

Having built a great career with significant accomplishments, Paul equates everything he has done to a pile of cow dung, all because of this one thing that he tells us he has found. Has Paul gone mad?

It's likely all of us have sympathy for Martha, feeling like at times we have been left alone to do the work God calls us to carry out. Mary sits at Jesus's feet and listens to him while her sister runs around. Is this really a commendable choice? After all, if we all chose to be Mary, nothing would get done! And what of Paul? Is it right to treat with disdain a lifetime of hard work, education, responsible labor, achievements, accomplishments, and productivity? Isn't that unnecessarily extreme?

This radical teaching found in both Luke and Philippians reflects the power of the temptation in our lives to compromise when it comes to this one thing that is needed. Everything in our life, *everything*, flows from this one thing, this first thing, this all-important and all-encompassing thing. Knowing Jesus Christ as our Lord will be, in the end, all that really matters in life and leadership. Everything else we think, say, and do will reflect the level of this knowing. Therefore, knowing must have our first, primary, and unequivocal allegiance. Jesus tells us that if we will seek him and his kingdom above all else, all the other things that would otherwise distract us will be taken care of. Do you believe that?

In a church I once visited, the congregants had framed a saying and hung it in the entryway. It read, "The Main Thing Is to Keep the Main Thing the Main Thing." Is the main thing in your life an unquenchable thirst and an unbridled drive to know Jesus Christ intimately and personally?

That is the one thing that is needed. As leaders, we must not miss this! If we do, we cannot be the leaders God has called us to be. We will miss the opportunity to lead as a steward and everything else in the life God created us to live. If, however, this is our priority, and we seek it with our whole heart, then we can trust in his promise that everything else will be taken care of by his loving hand.

How to Use It

The enemy wants to rob us of this relationship; how does he do this in your life? Being set free from this chain starts by identifying what is robbing us of intimacy and praying against each item. We pray to reject the temptation to allow the urgencies of the day to rob us of this one thing. This may mean choosing what we will *stop* doing to create the space and time for this intimacy to nurture in us.

Start by making a list of everything you believe is keeping you from experiencing the level of intimacy with God you (and he) desire. List the things that are time wasters, such as worry, social media, busy work, etc. Also list the distractions you allow to happen that compete for this time. Finally, write down the sins and temptations you have not acknowledged. These will block your passion for intimacy with your Lord.

Time wasters, distractions, temptations, and sins

_____

_____

_____

_____

_____

_____

_____

The next step is to prioritize those things that nurture the intimacy we so passionately want to have with Jesus. Is it a place or setting that helps you reconnect with God? Is it music, a devotional, a talk with a friend, a memory, or a piece of scripture? Name those things that create the desire and space for you to abide, listen, quiet your spirit, and seek after God's heart.

Finally, give permission to others to hold you accountable for this work. We cannot do this alone, at least not for long. Who cares for you enough to ask you about your time with Christ and about the priorities in your life? Who will be bold enough to challenge your distractions and call out your stagnancy? Find such a friend, an ally, and give them permission and opportunity to walk with you on this journey. As the proverb goes, "If you want to go fast, go alone. If you want to go far, go together." The journey of the faithful steward and steward leader is a long journey, and it requires companions who love us enough to hold us accountable.

This is a heavy chain; when Christ loosens that chain and lets it fall, you will enjoy rich intimacy with him and lead your people and your work in freedom and joy.

Reflection and Prayer

"I will pray each day that God would reveal to me the next deeper step he is calling me to take in my relationship to him and grant me the courage and faith to take it. My commitment is to name my biggest distraction as ———————————— and ask God each morning to give me the power to set it aside and find true intimacy with him."

"I keep asking that the God of our Lord Jesus Christ, the glorious Father, may give you the Spirit of wisdom and revelation, so that you may know him better." (Ephesians 1:17)

Key #4 – Our Identity
Is Secure in Jesus Christ

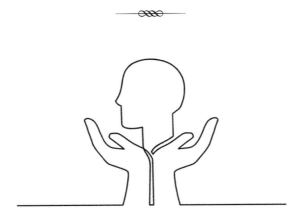

S teward leaders are ***secure in their identities in Jesus Christ***. They stand firm on that certainty and reject the temptation to desire affirmation or applause from any other source. This positions them to absorb criticism and deflect praise.

What Is at Stake

The link between our leadership and our identity cannot be overstated. As leaders, we will either find our identity solely in our new creation in Jesus Christ, or we will find it, at least some of it, in other, counterfeit sources. These may be our job, our title, or our reputation. The struggle here is between finding a solid footing for our self-image and the ability of the enemy to distract us through either pride or self-doubt. Let me explain by way of an illustration.

Picture yourself standing in the middle of a path with both

feet firmly on the ground, facing straight ahead, and fixing your eyes on your destination. When you keep to the center of the path and don't become distracted, you can work your way through obstacles, around rocks, through streams, and up steep grades, all without losing your focus on your destination. When our eyes are focused on Jesus Christ as our sole identity, then all that the world can offer us will not cause us to veer from the path.

Yet we do veer. We must recognize that the enemy wants us anywhere but walking the center of this path. He continually places before us enticements and challenges to move us off the path in one of two directions.

First, if he can get our eyes off Jesus, he can woo us to the left where, in our pride, we believe we can negotiate this path by ourselves. Pride always causes us to take our eyes off Jesus to look in some other, *any other*, location. Confident in ourselves and the strength of our leadership, we wander from the path and soon find ourselves out in the weeds. This desire to go it alone on our own strength motivated Moses to strike the rock. Remember the story,

> So, Moses took the staff from the LORD's presence, just as he commanded him. He and Aaron gathered the assembly together in front of the rock and Moses said to them, "Listen, you rebels, must we bring you water out of this rock?" Then Moses raised his arm and struck the rock twice with his staff. Water gushed out, and the community and their livestock drank. (Numbers 20:9–11)

As a frustrated leader, Moses took matters into his own hands and provided his people what they wanted, water. But rather than trusting God to provide, Moses became the provider for his people—a role that belongs to God and God alone. Moses was hailed the savior and deliverer as the children of Israel drank fully from the water that flowed from the rock. But that was not Moses's calling or work. Moses found himself off the path, having fixed his gaze someplace other than on his trust in God alone. And it cost Moses and the nation of Israel dearly.

As leaders, when we grab control of the situations in our life—or become too great in our own eyes, seeking to provide for our own needs and chart our own path—we deny our identity in Christ alone. Like Moses, we may produce short-term results, but we cannot please God, nor can we live our lives according to his purpose.

Are you leading from a place that is squarely in the center of the path to which God has called you? Are your eyes fixed on him every day? Or have you strayed off the path in your own pride and wandered from God's way due to your desire for control? Does your identity today rely on what you will do in your own power or on who you are as a child of God?

Remember, the enemy wants us anywhere but solidly in the center of the road to which God has called us. We have seen that he is thoroughly happy if, in our pride, we veer off the path to our left. In the other direction, he is just as happy if, in our despair, we career off the road to the right in our discouragement, believing the lie that we can't go it at all. Either way, the enemy is content. There is a consistent call in scripture for us not to be discouraged. The common theme is the refrain, "The Lord will be with you." We can only affirm this wonderful truth if our eyes remain fixed on Jesus. As soon as we look away from him, the challenges and trials of this life can overwhelm us. Even worse, when we look to ourselves to solve our own problems, we can meet with the kind of failure that will cause us to despair.

In an insidious way, our discouragement is more of a sign of our lack of trust in God than is our pride. The 2 Chronicles 20:15 passage declares, "The battle is not yours, but God's." Do we believe that? Do we believe that the one who leads us down the path of life is the one who has overcome? Do we believe that he has scouted the way, knowing that even the struggles and trials we will face on this path will end in victory because we follow the one who's already won the victory for us? The only way we can experience discouragement as leaders is by looking away from the face of the Son of God and letting the cares and concerns of our work rob us of the peace only he can offer.

This is the enemy's agenda—puffing us up in our pride or beating us down in discouragement. Whether we think more of ourselves or less of ourselves than we ought, we become ineffective as leaders in the kingdom of God. This is the chain we wear in our mistaken identity. If we are not set free from it, it will eventually bind us so tightly we will lose our calling and be crushed under its weight.

Understanding the Key

There is a sweet spot in the life of a steward leader. It is that place of stability, balance, and confidence where we are in the center of the path to which God has called us, our eyes fixed fully on him, and our stride steady and sure in his direction. We find that spot when we deny the enemy the opportunity to lie and deceive us into believing that we can go it alone or to discourage us from going at all.

Think about your day yesterday. What most controlled your decisions, your actions, your attitudes, your words, and your emotions? Was yesterday a day that was lived with your eyes fully fixed on Jesus Christ and your feet walking a path directly to him? If not, write down three things that you did yesterday that were symbolic of an overdependence on yourself or someone or something else. Once you have identified three things (decisions, actions, attitudes, words, emotions, etc.), acknowledge them before God and pray for the power to overcome the same temptations tomorrow. For they will be there waiting for you.

Where I have been overdependent on myself:

_____

_____

_____

_____

Second, where are your feet today? Your eyes? Your heart? Your identity? Think back to the last time you were really discouraged in your leadership role. You may not have to think far. Focus for a moment on the cause of your discouragement. Was it unknown to God? Was it greater than his ability to overcome it? Was it outside of the bounds of his love for you? You know the answer to all these is a resounding no! So what was the cause of your discouragement? Write it down and pray for God's power to overcome it tomorrow.

The cause of my discouragement:

_____

_____

Whether pride or discouragement, name it and surrender it back to Christ. Then stand firm on the solid path, eyes fixed on him, and lead from a place of confidence in who you are as a beloved and redeemed child of God.

How to Use It

Look for the patterns in your life as a leader that may indicate that you have veered off the path and tied your identity to some source other than Christ. Look at this chart; do any of these descriptors match your self-image today?

Puffed up with Pride	*Beaten Down and Discouraged*
Seeking the approval of others	Fear of criticism
Needing to be liked	Believing we're misunderstood
Needing to be needed	Feeling useless, a failure
Propping up our reputation	Resentment at correction
Needing to get the credit	Doubting our own work

If so, here are four *musts* to start following immediately:

1. We *must* reject the temptation of pride, which is to desire affirmation or applause from any other source. Where do I look for applause in my role as a leader?
2. We *must* reject the temptation to tie our reputation or identity to anything other than who we are in Jesus Christ.
3. We *must* distinguish between who we are in Christ and the roles he may call us to play in life and leadership.
4. We *must* pray for God to set us free to find our identity in him alone, so that we are able to encourage others and lift others up.

Now make two lists. On the first, list everything you can think of that completes this sentence: *"I am a child of God, and in his eyes, I am…"* Consider how God sees his children in scripture. Consider things like *loved, fearfully and wonderfully made, holy, and precious.*

"I am a child of God, and in his eyes, I am…"

_____

_____

_____

_____

On the second, list the things you believe about yourself that are not in line with the first list. These can be negative, like *worthless, failure, incapable, insecure, and fearful.* These can also be false places where you find your identity instead of in Christ alone, such as *successful ministry leader, great preacher, well regarded in my community, famous author, great parent, etc.*

Lies I am believing:

_____

_____

_____

_____

Finally, circle the *one* view in the second list you most want to surrender and stop believing about yourself.

Reflection and Prayer

"I will begin each day affirming the balance God seeks in my self-image and pray not to be pulled in either direction. I will surrender my identity back to God each day, refuse to play the owner, and take on the mantle of the steward of every area of my life. My commitment is to name and pray against the false identity of _____ and trust God to keep my eyes on him and my identity secure in the knowledge that I am a child of God."

> See what great love the Father has lavished on us, that we should be called children of God! And that is what we are! (1 John 3:1)

Key #5 – People Are Ends and Not Means

Steward leaders see those they lead and serve as fellow pilgrims. They shun the temptation to use others to further their own agendas. Consequently, they encourage the personal and spiritual growth of those they lead and with whom they serve.

What Is at Stake

Each of us have a personal and professional agenda. We have goals and dreams, things we believe we must accomplish to be successful. We are busy, on a mission, engaged, and in pursuit of achievement. What happens when we encounter other people while charging ahead to meet our objectives?

If we are not careful, our desire to achieve our agenda can mean treating other people whom God puts in our path as means to our own ends. In Jesus's great commandment, we are told we must love our neighbor as we love ourself (Luke 10:27).

In our third key, we learned the freedom of finding our identity in Christ and how in doing so, we can truly love ourselves as his beloved children. With our identity restored, we can now embrace the call to love our neighbor in the same freedom we have in loving ourselves. This means we are free to see our relationships with others as ends in themselves, and not as means to some other purpose. This is a lot harder than it may sound.

Try to think of a relationship (not a relative) in which you have invested a great deal of your own time, energy, and emotion, and yet from which you have received almost nothing in return. Or worse, where the response was negative. Are you still in it? How often have you remained in a relationship regardless of any positive response on their part? Can you think of one? It is difficult to care about another person in a relationship without receiving anything in return. Taking a more realistic approach, think of the relationships that have waned or died out altogether. How many of them failed because the investment of time, energy, and emotion brought you little in return? We may not want to admit it, but we affix an expected *return on investment* to each relationship we enter. If the return is not realized, we can be tempted to shift our investments to relationships with more potential.

The root of the problem is the bondage we have to our own self-interest. As long as we look to relationships to meet our needs or further our progress toward our own objectives, they will always be measured for their usefulness to us. For a leader, this is a powerful bondage. This chain weighs heavily on the shoulders of a leader who only values people for what they can help him or her accomplish.

This bondage can also go beyond our life as a leader and make its way into our marriages, our roles as parents, our friendships, and our church. Owner-leaders see people as either stepping-stones to be used on their way to building their own kingdoms or obstacles to that same kingdom-building pursuit. They are two sides of the same coin. This may sound harsh, but unless we drive the owner-leader temptation from our leadership, we will inevitably fall into the desire to control others for our own advantage. Whether we see people as means to our ends, or as obstacles to our pursuit of those ends, much is at stake when we choose to carry this heavy chain.

Understanding the Key

We will not make the shift from "relationships as means" to "relationships as ends" until we are personally set free. To view our relationships as ends and not means requires presence. We must be *with* people to be in relationship with them. And this requires a prioritization of time, a commitment to involvement, and selflessness about our intentions and our desired outcomes.

This gift of presence beckons us into life as community. And not just as individuals meeting together, but with a deeper sense of interdependence and mutual accountability and trust. If we are the body of Christ, we are called to rely on one another, sacrifice for our neighbors' well-being, and invest ourselves in community. We are called to reclaim the virtue and joy of sacrifice for one another and rediscover the gift and ministry of presence in a time-starved, individualistic world.

The key is our freedom to look beyond our own needs, because God is our provider. If we are confident in God's provision, if our identity is secure in him, then we are free to invest in others. We will see them, like ourselves, as someone on a journey to experience greater freedom and joy. We will cheer them on as they, too, see chains drop off. We will use the intersection of our journey with theirs to be used by God to help them along the way. We will do this because we are free to do so.

Ask yourself, are you free in your relationship with the people around you? Do you practice the gift of presence, taking the time to be in community with your neighbor? Can you set aside your agenda and focus away from your needs to better love and lead and encourage the relationships God has given you as a gift to steward? This is real freedom, and God can work through you in powerful ways to impact the lives of everyone you lead if you rely on him to be your provider and look to how he can use you to bring freedom into the lives of the people in your life.

How to Use It

One powerful example of exercising freedom at this level is considering whether you are trying to mold the people you lead into shapes and forms that will best help you accomplish your goals, or whether you are partnering with God, asking him to work through you to unfold them to be more fully the person he created them to be? Unfolding and not molding is one way to use this key to unlock not only your chain, but the chains worn by others.

A second way is by simply joining the journey of others and being sensitive to their agenda. What are their needs and how might God use you to be an answer to their prayers? As leaders, if we concentrated more on helping our employees or fellow workers experience the abundant life in Christ, we would see our places of work flourish as never before. This means seeing them as God sees them. It calls us to steward every relationship and every interaction as gifts. It requires that God cultivate in us the awareness that everyone around us are fellow travelers.

Here are three ways to live this out:

1. Pray that God would use you to help each person you encounter along your way in their journey of becoming more faithful stewards.
2. Resist the temptation to use others to further your own agendas.
3. Die to your need to be needed, to always be right, and to have the last word.

Here's an important exercise to help you see how this is lived out in your own life. Select three people who are close to you; a family member, a coworker, and a friend. For each one, do an honest assessment of three things. First, how do you actually view them, as someone through whom you can get your own needs met or truly as an end in themselves? Do you focus on their needs even at the cost of your own? Second, where are they on their journey of becoming a faithful steward, and do you know? Have you asked about and listened to and understood the journey they're on with Jesus, and have you prayed how God might use you to help them on that journey? Third, what personal encouragement could you give them the next time you meet that might help advance their own steward journey?

In these ways, by focusing on these types of questions for all our relationships, God can set us free in our leadership to unfold the potential of the people we serve.

Reflection and Prayer

"I will begin each day with a prayer that God would enable me to see my neighbors and coworkers as he sees them. I will ask for the heart to join them on their journey and be used by God to bless, encourage, and challenge them in ways that are in line with his will for them. My commitment is to take action as God leads to ask forgiveness and, with God's help, change my attitude toward _____ , _____ , and _____ , and begin to walk with them as fellow travelers."

> We who are strong ought to bear with the failings of the weak and not to please ourselves. Each of us should please our neighbors for their good, to build them up. (Romans 15:1–2)

Key #6 – All Resources Are Gifts from an Abundant God

S teward leaders *regard all resources as gifts from God*. They resist the temptation to hoard or waste them. Instead, they put them to work consistent with instructions in God's word and the leading of the Holy Spirit, and they do this for God's glory.

What Is at Stake

In the first section of this book, we named how the journey from two-kingdom bondage to one-kingdom freedom was an issue of lordship. In our kingdom, we are the lord. When we surrender all our life back to Christ, we acknowledge his lordship of everything. Just to be clear, he always was Lord of everything! Our journey is simply a continual acknowledgment and surrender of those things we pretend to own so that we might experience the real freedom that comes from being a one-kingdom steward.

At the heart of this battle for lordship is our relationship with the created things in the world. In this level of our relationships, we include time, the gifts and skills God has given us, the resources he has provided us, and the created world itself. In each of these areas, there are three temptations we face as leaders.

1. *The temptation to be our own provider.* This is the norm in a world that celebrates independence and rewards those who are self-made, financially successful leaders. We are taught from a young age that we are to look out for ourselves, be responsible and provide for our own needs, and later, provide for the needs of our family. So what is at stake in this temptation to be our own provider? At one level, there is nothing wrong with working hard, providing for our needs, and providing for the needs of the people we love. In fact, it is commended in scripture. This is not a suggestion that we embrace an entitlement mentality. Exactly the opposite. The temptation to be our own provider takes us beyond the means that God has given us to work hard and earn a living and seeks to replace it with a distorted sense of believing that all that we earn, all that we buy, and all that we amass really does come, ultimately, from our own hard work and efforts. It effectively cuts God out of the picture. When we see ourselves as the true provider, we will be thrown back into a mode of self-reliance, which results in our leadership becoming our work, done our way, and for our glory.

Let's return to the story of Moses striking the rock to bring water for his people. God commanded him to strike the rock once and trust that God would provide. The glory was to be God's alone. But listen now to how a frustrated leader chose to act:

He and Aaron gathered the assembly together in front of the rock and Moses said to them, "Listen, you rebels, must we bring you water out of this rock?" Then Moses raised his arm and struck the rock twice with his staff. Water gushed out, and the community and their livestock drank.

But the LORD said to Moses and Aaron, "Because you did not trust in me enough to honor me as holy in the sight of the Israelites, you will not bring this community into the land I give them." (Numbers 20:10–12)

Moses shifted the focus from God's provision to his own: "Must *we* bring you water out of this rock?" The result was the opportunity to lead Israel into the Promised Land. Listen to these other warnings of the downfall of self-reliance:

In 2 Chronicles 26:16, King Uzziah's pride and fame were growing, and so was his self-reliance. "But when he was strong his heart was lifted up, to his destruction."

In Psalm 147:10–11, we are reminded what the Lord values and what he does not: "He does not delight in the strength of the horse; He takes no pleasure in the legs of a man. The LORD takes pleasure in those who fear Him, In those who hope in His mercy."

The prophet Jeremiah warned against self-reliance in chapter 17 verse 5: "Thus says the LORD: 'Cursed is the man who trusts in man and makes flesh his strength, Whose heart departs from the LORD.'"

The prophet Hosea warned likewise: "'You have plowed wickedness; You have reaped iniquity. You have eaten the fruit of lies, because you trusted in your own way, in the multitude of your mighty men'" (Hosea 10:13).

These are just a few of so many examples and warnings in scripture about the downfall of relying on our own strength instead of on God's power and provision. Owner-leaders have no other option but to trust in their own leadership expertise and exercise their own control to bring about success. It is a dead-end way to lead.

The steward leader will always look beyond every provision to the ultimate provider and see God's hand in everything. Steward leaders work hard and set high bars for excellence, but they never lose sight of the fact that every good thing that comes to us is from the hand of God. They have the ability to invest their skills and expertise in doing great work while always seeing God's abundant provision in everything. As steward leaders, we must work hard to maintain that balance and never be tempted by the desire to see ourselves as the ultimate provider for our own needs, for the needs of our family, or for the needs of organizations we lead.

2. *The temptation for misplaced security.* This second temptation is all about trust. As followers of Jesus, we will always be asked to put our full trust and security in him. As leaders of organizations, businesses, churches, and ministries, we are constantly challenged to provide security for the organizations we lead and the people we serve. This, too often, comes in the form of financial reserves, endowments, elimination of debt, and the creation of strong fundraising programs. It is important to say here that all these are important tools for every ministry. There is nothing wrong with any of them inherently, but there lurks behind them the opportunity to fall prey to this second temptation. This happens when we put our security in the accumulation of resources and seek after a sense of well-being in our financial position. This requires honesty and careful self-reflection. How much of your own personal security do you find in the size of your savings, your retirement plan, or the wealth you've accumulated? In

the same way, to what extent has your organization sought after its security in some or all of these ways?

Out of this misplaced security comes the deeper evil of the love of money. When we treasure the security that money brings us, it will become our master. This is a deep and evil root that can easily take hold in our life and leadership.

On a recent trip to India, I sat under some powerful teachings on generosity. One speaker drew a diagram of a plant with a deep root system. He circled the roots and referred to 1 Timothy 6:9–10:

> Those who want to get rich fall into temptation and a trap and into many foolish and harmful desires that plunge people into ruin and destruction. For the love of money is a root of all kinds of evil. Some people, eager for money, have wandered from the faith and pierced themselves with many griefs.

He stated bluntly that if, in our repentance, we continually only deal with the visible part of our sin that grows above the ground, we will never get to the root. Paul identifies that root as the love of money, from which all kinds of evils spring up in our life. The first step at this level of becoming a steward leader is to take seriously the entangled root system that exists in our lives and in our institutions because of our love of money and all it represents. True repentance for a steward leader means doing the hard work of digging deep and pulling out these embedded roots.

It does little good to repent of our lack of trust in God to be our provider if we do not also understand that the root of that mistrust is a deep-seated desire to hold on to and trust in financial security instead. We can repent of the sins of envy and jealousy; however, they will never be fully defeated until we dig out the root of the love of possessions and the place they hold in our lives as we compare ourself to others. We can wish against this temptation, but to root it out requires earnest prayer and accountability to defeat our dependence on the things of this world and cut off the desire to tie our image and reputation to what we accumulate.

As a steward leader, what are you called to do today to begin the process of digging deeply into the values and culture of your organization to identify the root system that is your love, reliance, dependence, and desire for money and the security it brings you? What will it take to remove those roots from your institutional heart and replace them with rich soil in which the Spirit of God can lead you and your people into a new time of trust, dependence, and surrender to God through Jesus Christ?

The challenge here is ultimately one of trust. If we truly trust God to be our provider, then the fullness of our security in this world must be in him and his role as our faithful provider. The enemy will work in our organizations and in our hearts to entice us to give lip service to God, while seeing our real sense of contentment and security in other things. Steward leaders watch for this carefully, challenge it when they see it, pray over it in their own hearts, and seek to lead their organizations to steer clear of these misplaced securities and bring them back to their only firm foundation and God alone.

3. *The third temptation is to view God's resources through the lens of scarcity and not abundance.* We live in a world that is motivated by what we lack. Our desire to accumulate wealth, fame, and power are driven by the conviction that whatever we have, whatever God has provided us today, is not enough.

The secret to happiness is... more. The enemy uses this scarcity mindset to breed in us a whole array of bondages, including envy (others have more), fear (what if I lose what I have?), drivenness (having more is the answer to my problems), and our misunderstood idea of success. This scarcity worldview takes leaders to some very unhealthy places on their journey. Among other effects, if we lead from scarcity and operate as owners, we can be tempted to:

a. Protect "our" donors, fearing that others may steal them away and our ministry might lose out. We see this in far too many pastors who are reluctant to allow their congregation to learn about new ministries, for fear that they will start giving to them and give less to the church;

b. Resent employees who leave for other positions, charging disloyalty and fearing we may not be able to replace them;

c. Push for growth out of belief that we never have enough facilities, staff, or resources to do our work;

d. Breed a culture of discontentment, seldom celebrating success, but always pushing for further achievement and larger goals;

e. Envy other organizations and ministries when they receive a large grant, donation, or other blessing; and

f. See other organizations, ministries, or churches as competition, and measuring success by how we measure up.

These are just some of the ugly outcomes of a leader's heart that views resources through a lens of scarcity.

Understanding the Key

Steward leaders deal with stuff well. This should make sense to us at this point in our journey. Once we have been set free to lead, we can treat others as ends and invest resources as careful caretakers of what God has entrusted to us for our use. Having rejected the temptation to play the owner, we can trust God to be our provider and handle his resources with integrity and grace. This includes our time, our skills, and our finances. It also includes our care for God's creation. All of these flow easily and freely from the heart of a steward leader.

One good test is to ask yourself where your true security lies? We can be tempted as leaders to place our security in human performance and financial strength, and both will fail us. Steward leaders embrace an abundance mentality, believing that God will supply all their needs according to his glorious riches in Christ Jesus (Philippians 4). They place their security in God's promises of provision and lead their people to embrace that same freedom. This will be reflected in:

- Our handling of time; submitting back to him all twenty-four hours he has gifted to us and seeking his leading for how we best invest it for the kingdom.
- Our handling of our skills, talents, and experiences; seeking to use the fullest of how God created us and the people we lead in his work for his glory.
- Our handling of our financial resources; committed to being faithful to God's leading in how we earn them, spend them, invest them, and give them, and praying against all temptation to hoard them or waste them.
- Our care for his creation; seeking to be faithful stewards of our earth and its environment and resources.

In these ways, God will set us free to lead, to take risks and to invest his resources abundantly in his work for his glory.

Try this little exercise and see if it helps you identify the unwanted roots in your organization. Meet with your leadership team and finish this sentence for your organization: "We demonstrate our love of money when we..." Write down as many phrases you can think of that complete that sentence for you. Here are a few for starters. "We demonstrate our love of money when we envy what other organizations have, tie our identity to what we own and how much we raise or earn, worry about whether we will have enough money to be sustainable, choose to keep and protect money more than invest and use it in God's work, and invest the majority of our working life talking about it." Will you be honest with yourself and make your own organizational list? That is the first step to digging out the deep roots of the love of money, misplaced security, and scarcity in your culture.

We demonstrate our love for money when we...

_____

_____

_____

_____

For the steward leader, the key is recognizing these temptations and surrendering all God's resources back to him for his use and his glory.

Reflection and Prayer

"I will begin each morning submitting my time, talents, and resources to God's work. I will pray for the heart and vision to lead a lifestyle that reflects a love and care for God's creation. My commitment is to surrender these three things that I view with a scarcity mindset, _____ , _____ and _____ , and ask God to replace that view with an abundance attitude, investing them in his work, confident that he has given me enough for the work he called me to do."

And my God will meet all your needs according to the riches of his glory in Christ Jesus. (Philippians 4:19)

Key #7 – We Must Be Prepared for the Spiritual Battle

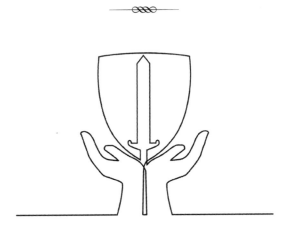

S teward leaders *recognize the spiritual battle they are in as they strive to lead as faithful stewards in a world of people playing the role of master.* They speak the truth, which sets people free from bondage so they may experience abundant life.

What Is at Stake

There are two forces at work in the universe. One is all-powerful and promises to give us life, freedom, and peace. The other is a parasite, seeking to steal our peace, enslave us, and destroy our life. We live in a world at war against us whose outcome is already determined. Yet that does not make the battle any less real or the enemy any less powerful or threatening. In fact, the certainty of the outcome serves only to infuriate and motivate the enemy to deceive us all the more. He wants as much collateral damage as possible.

The most heinous form of this deception is the enemy's power to convince us that there is no real battle going on at all. Many leaders are uncomfortable talking about things like warfare, weapons, battlefields, and victory. "Onward, Christian Soldiers" has become a forgotten hymn from a bygone age. Such is the power of this deception. And it will continue to blind us as long as God's people refrain from reading God's word. You see, the Bible is a book about warfare from beginning to end. There was warfare before creation, warfare in the garden, warfare throughout the Old Testament, warfare surrounding the birth of Jesus, warfare during his entire ministry, warfare in Gethsemane, warfare on the cross, warfare at the founding of the church, warfare throughout the book of Acts, warfare that followed Paul, and warfare right down to the last chapter of Revelation. To deny the spiritual battle we face, we must ignore the major themes of scripture, close our ears to a significant amount of Jesus's teachings, and reject a central truth of human experience that is lived out from Genesis to Revelation.

If warfare and our spiritual battle are such central themes to God's story of creation, salvation, and final glory, how prepared are you to enter into the battle as a steward leader on behalf of your people?

The aspect of this warfare that concerns us most specifically as leaders is the battle for our freedom. Paul tells us, "It is for freedom that Christ has set us free. Stand firm, then, and do not let yourselves be burdened again by a yoke of slavery" (Galatians 5:1). That is the strategy of the enemy, to reenslave us in our leadership work even after we've been set free. He does it by lying to us about our relationship with Christ, our true identity, our need to succeed, the importance of our agenda, the value of reputation, and the purpose of our role as a leader. He uses our ignorance and inattentiveness against us. When we lose sight of God's word and become distracted by the challenges of our role, we are easy prey for the lies and lures of the hater of our souls.

God calls us to put on his full armor and wade into this battle (Ephesians 6:10–20). We must fight against the forces that seek to enslave us again. God created us for freedom. Christ set us free. And by the power of the Holy Spirit, we protect and advance that freedom as the army of the kingdom of God. If we shrink back from battle language, we have already lost the war.

It is for freedom that Christ has set you free. That freedom must be fought for every day. That is the calling of the steward leader who has been set free to lead. We must take up our cross and wade into the battle, knowing we will be victorious, because greater is he that is in us than he that is in the world (1 John 4:4).

Are you engaged in this great cosmic battle? Are you prepared for it?

The battle we fight as steward warriors in each of these four areas of relationships is being waged right in front of us every day. We don't have to go looking for this conflict—it is brought to our door and thrown in our face almost constantly. From the attacks on our intimacy with God to assaults on our self-image, to the enmity between us and our neighbor, and to a gnawing sense of anxiety and urgency regarding money, maintaining our freedom as a steward leader requires daily vigilance. If we let down our guard for a moment, the old nature within us will rise up and entice us to play the owner once again. Remember the words of Paul: "Stand firm, then, and do not let yourselves be burdened again by a yoke of slavery" (Galatians 5:1).

It is not enough just to maintain our own freedom. We were set free to lead our people to that same freedom. The most powerful expression of that freedom will come from how we lead. Our actions will speak loudly to the extent that God has transformed our hearts into that of a steward leader. The great preacher and theologian Charles Haddon Spurgeon said, as recounted by David Jeremiah in *Turning Points: Finding Moments of Refuge in the Presence of God*, "A man's life is always more forcible than his speech. When men take stock of him, they reckon his deeds as dollars and his words as pennies. If his life and doctrine disagree, the mass of onlookers accept his practice and reject his preaching."[15]

Understanding the Key

The work of a steward leader is radically different when you operate from a position of freedom in a world in bondage. I pray that you will begin leading in this revolutionary freedom more every day. It is yours as a child of God and heir to the promise of salvation. It is yours as an image bearer of our creator, God, and a caretaker of his good creation. It is yours to bear witness to the truth of God's sovereignty over and love for all creation. It is yours as a faithful steward set free to lead.

Claim that freedom for yourself in the victorious name of Jesus. And lead in the power of the Holy Spirit to the glory of the Father.

How to Use It

We must take seriously the battle we enter as we try to live and lead as faithful stewards. If we are to be engaged in this great battle, we must create a battle plan. As you complete your five commitments, they will become your plan of attack as you seek

---

15 David Jeremiah, *Turning Points: Finding Moments of Refuge in the Presence of God* (Nashville: Thomas Nelson, 2006), 18

to live as a steward leader in a world of owner-leaders. Your plan will help you:

- Be aware of the ways the enemy deceives and lies to you regarding your ownership desires;
- Meditate on scriptures that equip you for spiritual battle, putting on the full armor of God;
- Fight this battle together, in community; and
- Live into the truth that the battle belongs to the Lord and victory is already secured in Jesus Christ.

As part of your plan, complete the following exercise. Create two lists, labeling the first list "Scriptures that encourage me" and labeling the second list "Allies that will fight beside me." Fill out the first list with scripture verses that challenge and inspire you in the battle. On the second list, identify the key allies you can trust to fight alongside you. Finally, pray over each column that God would keep these scriptures in the front of your mind and that he would help you encourage your allies in this battle.

Scriptures

_____

_____

_____

_____

Allies

_____

_____

_____

_____

Reflection and Prayer

If Christ is setting you free in relationship to the things of this world, you should be able to look back at your attitudes and habits before this emancipation and look ahead at a very different landscape for your life as a leader. Is there a stark difference between the two? If not, pray each day for that freedom to overwhelm your spirit and set you free. If there is a demonstrable difference, write down three areas where your newfound freedom is being lived out in your leadership. Then ask yourself if others might see this difference. If so, how can you be ready to give an account for the change that has taken place within you which has produced this fruit? Seek the Spirit's guidance and be prepared. For if the evidence is clear to see, people will ask. Will you be ready to answer?

"Gracious and loving heavenly Father, thank you for having won for me the great victory over death and evil. I claim that victory for my life in the name of Jesus Christ. I know that even though the outcome is determined, I am still to be engaged in the battle every day. I confess that I don't feel prepared or equipped to do so. My faith seems so weak that it is hard for me to imagine myself as a warrior. But you have promised that all things are possible through Christ who gives us strength. I need that strength, Lord, because by myself, I will fail in the future, as I have in the past. I am sensing the freedom that you want for me. I have felt chains fall off me throughout this study. I have experienced my anxiety and fear turning to trust and peace. I don't want to lose this, Lord. I don't want to go back and be enslaved again by all of the bondage that I used to carry. So, I am willing to fight, to be part of the army of the kingdom of God, and to enter into the battle in your name. But I will do so only through your power and with the strength that comes from you. Prepare me, Lord, for this work. Grant me the courage to step out boldly and, with faith, claim the victory of the steward leader in your name. Amen."

Victory Begins with Surrender

We can summarize these seven keys with this one powerful statement: ***Steward leaders have learned that victory begins with surrender***. They set aside the temptation of self-reliance and take on the mantle of a leader of no reputation. Only after surrendering can a steward lead effectively.

What Is at Stake

This summary takes us back to where we started—"It's all his." This is the cry of joyful surrender that sets us free. As you consider your own journey in reading through this book, I ask you:

- Have you moved away from the bondage of self-reliance and found the freedom in placing your full trust in God alone?
- Have you relinquished control in your life and leadership and released everything back to him?
- Have you named the ownership tendencies in your leadership and assumed the posture of the faithful steward in their place?
- Have you named the causes of spiritual stagnation that are damaging your intimacy with Christ, and are you recommitted to making the pursuit of intimacy with Christ as your highest calling?
- Have you confessed the sources of misplaced identity and found your sole identity in Christ alone?

- Have you repented of the ways you have used relationships with others for your own ends and found new freedom in relying on God for the strength to love your neighbor as you love yourself?
- Have you identified where you have become complacent in your stewardship of God's resources and creation and examined every aspect of your life for the faithful stewarding of all God's resources for his glory?
- Have you experienced the victory over fear and apathy in the leadership battle, seeking to be empowered by God to enter the battle as a warrior who is ready to be used by God to speak truth and help others be set free?

These are the key questions that will guide your journey from owner-leader bondage to steward leader freedom.

The road to victory begins with absolute surrender. The journey of the faithful, obedient steward leader is fraught with the same paradoxes as the journey of the disciple of Jesus. They are, in fact, the exact same journey. In both, we find life by losing it, receive by giving, lead by serving, become first by being last, and are exalted by being humble. For steward leaders, this means we are victorious by surrendering. This sounds absurd, but it is the heart of everything we have said in this little book. We must understand this simple truth about the battle in which we are engaged if we are to have the hope for victory.

This one truth of the power of surrender can be read back into everything we have said:

- It's all God's, and we are called to surrender our desire to play the owner and embrace our role as the faithful steward set free to lead.

- We are one-kingdom people, and we must surrender the role of lord over our own second kingdom and place everything under the one lordship of Jesus Christ.
- We are given the gift of intimacy with God in Christ, and we must surrender the insatiable drive we have to be doers and allow God to free us to serve as steward leaders.
- We are given the gift of confidence, and we must surrender our pride that would have us find our identity and freedom in anything but in Christ alone.
- We are given the gift of presence with our neighbor, and we must surrender the desire to use our people as means to our own ends and be set free to see them as Christ sees them.
- We are given the gift of nurture of creation, and we must surrender the deceptive ideas that we find security in earthly things or rule creation for our own gain and instead become the caretakers that God created us to be.
- We are called into the great battle for freedom, and we will only be victorious if we fully surrender our will and ways to God, allowing him to work through us to set others free.

Reflection and Prayer

My sincerest prayer is that in some small way over the course of this journey you have come to know the freedom of surrender for yourself. I pray that chains have fallen, that the lies of the enemy have been discovered, and the truth and beauty of the love of God has been experienced at a deeper level. May the Lord of freedom be your Lord and deliverer, your strength, and your comfort for the battle that lies ahead. And every day may you know the peace that comes from the unchained life and the joy that flows from the heart that is genuinely free.

Part 3

YOUR PERSONAL BATTLE PLAN

A Tale of Two Spirals

In this book, we have introduced you to the following steward leader principles:

1. Becoming a leader of no reputation
2. One-kingdom versus two-kingdom leadership
3. Four levels of relationships: with God, self, neighbor, and creation
4. Life on all four levels as a gift to be stewarded
5. Success as faithfulness
6. Owner-leaders versus steward leaders
7. The seven keys that mark the life of a steward leader

We want to bring these principles together now and conclude by showing how they work in the life of a Christian leader. To do so, we will use the image of two spirals. When we think of spirals, we start at one point and follow a progression that circles around on itself and either moves upward or downward, depending on the content. Upward spirals allow us to build on our experiences in an ever more positive and progressive way toward the achievement of ultimate goals. Downward spirals feed on each other in an ever increasingly destructive way, leading to failure.

The key is understanding how they feed on each other. They are not independent attitudes and actions, but an interrelated pattern of behavior that will either drive us into an ever more debilitating bondage or free us for greater kingdom impact.

Both spirals begin at the same place. They start with our decision to view life through the lens of either an owner or a steward. These spirals begin for us every day, every morning, as we look out at our life and the demands of our leadership roles and make the decision whether we will serve in them as owners or stewards. From this one simple decision, we will begin down the path of either the upward or downward spiral.

The Downward Spiral

What was the first thing that came to mind this morning when you woke up, when you looked out on the day and had your first thoughts of your agenda, your meetings, the responsibilities you faced, and the challenges before you? It is certain that you responded with either the heart of an owner or a steward. Let's look at what happens when our first inclination is to grab ahold of ownership and the belief that we need to control the things that are before us. What is at stake when we start our day believing that if we are to achieve our definition of success it is up to us?

The first step along the path of the downward spiral is this attitude of an owner-leader. We may not use this exact language or state it in such clear terms, but when we feel the anxiety, fear, and stress of our leadership role, it is certain that we're taking this ownership viewpoint. Once we do so, the next step will be to look to ourselves and others for answers and solutions to the problems and challenges we face. Because we believe that we are ultimately owners in charge of fixing these things, we will rely primarily on our own strength and that of our fellow workers to solve these problems. Self-reliance is the default of the owner-leader. This sets us on a course of doing our work our way, even if we believe that it's ultimately for God's glory.

The next step follows closely on the heels of this choice for self-reliance. If we are to rely on our own skills and strengths to solve our problems, based on our belief that we are owners, then it will be easy for the enemy to disconnect us from the need to pray and seek God's guidance over the work that we do. This may be subtle. It may come in the form of being too busy for prayer and devotional time or too distracted to focus when we do. Our time with God in devotion and prayer may become stale, and as a result, we may struggle to find the space for it in our busy schedule. Whatever the cause, we will find ourselves losing our sense of closeness and intimacy with Christ, replacing it with quick and efficient prayers that allow us to get on to the work we know we need to do. Self-reliance will always inhibit our ability to cultivate deep intimacy with Christ. It will throw us back on ourselves to get to work and solve problems on our own. After all, we are the owner, right?

The next step down this spiral is to define success in terms of the accomplishment of our work. There's that term again, *our work*. An ownership mindset built upon self-reliance will define success as what we are able to accomplish using metrics of tangible growth and worldly success. Having lost our sense of intimacy with Christ, this misplaced definition of success is able to overwhelm us and consume everything we do.

From the steps of self-reliance, a loss of intimacy with Christ, and a definition of success as productivity and accomplishment, it becomes all too easy for us to tie our identity to our work. After all, we have defined it as *our work*. In this next step, we look for affirmation and a sense of self-worth in our job, our title, and our reputation. We know deep inside we are children of God, but what drives us is career success, because we have placed our entire identity upon it.

Here is the downward spiral to this point: an ownership mindset cultivates an attitude of self-reliance, which robs us of intimacy with Christ, focuses success on accomplishment, and ties our identity to what we do, rather than who we are. From here, the next two deathly steps are all too easy.

On this downward spiral, we now consider the relationships we have with authorities, peers, and those who report to us. As owner-leaders, how do we respond? Quite simply, if this is our work, and our identity and definition of success are tied to it, then people must be means to the ends of our success. In other words, we need people to do the things we need them to do in order for us to be successful. And our success determines our identity, so the stakes are high. Without even meaning to do so, we can become manipulative and coercive in our relationships. People become either the way in which we accomplish our goals or obstacles to that happening. What is lost is seeing people as they are, as God sees them. Instead, every interaction carries with it the question of a return on investment. "Am I getting out of this relationship what I need to in order to achieve my goals?" Again, this is subtle. It's not something we do overtly, but it becomes the heart and attitude of owner-leaders who have descended to this point on the downward spiral.

The final step is understandable and unavoidable. Owner-leaders will now look to all the resources around them and ask how they can be used to help them achieve success. Whether it be time, the talents and skills of people around them, financial resources, or even the creation itself, all these will be seen by owner-leaders as resources at their disposal to help them achieve what they must achieve to maintain their identity and prop up their self-worth. If you are operating like an owner-leader, you will recognize these attitudes toward resources. Issues of money, time, and the skills of the people around you will be sources of stress and conflict. Decisions in each of these areas will be made according to bottom line results and return on investment. Everything will be measured by your definition of success externally and your need for the applause of the people around you and recognition for accomplishments for your identity internally.

This, then, is the bottom of the downward spiral. It is a place of high pressure, a drive to succeed that can ruin marriages, health, and Christian witness. It produces constant stress and a gnawing anxiety that no matter how much you do, it's never enough. It breeds a quiet sense of fear of failure and a final resignation to despair that leadership is just not what you expected it to be. From this place near the bottom of this spiral, leaders are in great danger of moral failings, ethical compromise, depression, and total burnout.

When we work with leaders who have reached this point on the spiral, the most common question they ask is, "How did I get here?" They're looking for one bad decision or one hurtful experience for the answer. However, we help them retrace their steps back up the spiral to that point where they viewed their life through the lens of an owner and took the next steps toward self-reliance, leading them to the most damaging step on this journey: the loss of intimacy with Christ. From that point, the treacherous journey down this spiral is almost inevitable.

Are you on this downward journey? If so, it's time to climb back up to the beginning and start your new journey upward toward the abundant life God created you to live.

The Upward Spiral

We are back at that moment at the beginning of each day when you make a decision on how you will view all the life that lies before you. This time, we will choose a different path. Imagine starting each day by looking out at everything that represents the entirety of your life and leadership and proclaiming over all of it, "it's all God's." This is the morning prayer of the steward leader. This is a recognition and proclamation that all life is a gift, having been redeemed and given back to you in Christ, that you now have the supreme privilege of stewarding for the sake of the true owner. From this standpoint, the only logical question to ask is this, "What would the owner have me do with all that is his?"

By asking this simple question, the leader affirms his place in one kingdom and proclaims only one Lord over that kingdom. This is a declaration of independence! It is freedom to set aside our self-life, our desire to own and control, and our belief that somehow there's more happiness and joy in our kingdom than in God's. By declaring his lordship over everything, we surrender the entirety of life and every second of our day as leaders to be used for his purposes and his glory.

The next step from here leads us to experience God's perfect joy. If everything belongs to God and if our driving passion is to faithfully steward what is his, then we will willingly adopt a posture of prayer to ask the true owner how he would have us live our day. Prayer, scripture, and devotion are now the fuel with which we can produce true fruit for the kingdom of God. They are the very life breath of the steward leader. As a result, steward leaders only get off their knees when they sense they have a clear understanding of how the owner would have them care for and invest his resources in the work of his kingdom. Deepening this intimacy with Christ becomes the single most important calling of a steward leader. It starts with an attitude of total surrender and ends with a mandate, a calling, and a vision for how they live their day.

From deep intimacy with Christ will come the definition of success as faithfulness. By setting aside the self-life and focusing their attention on Christ and his vision for their work, steward leaders realign all their expectations and metrics, orienting these on the passionate pursuit of knowing God's will and doing it with excellence. They set their goals, manage their people, adjust their strategies, and make their decisions according to this north star.

With faithfulness as their driving passion, steward leaders immerse themselves in their work, knowing that, as important as it may be and as committed to it as they are, it is never theirs. And because it belongs to God, so does their identity. This next step of keeping their identity solely focused in Jesus Christ allows the steward leader to take risks and make decisions according to God's leading. Steward leaders carry out their work according to a 1 Corinthians 3 formula. In that text, Paul says, "I plant, Apollos waters, but God brings the increase." Steward leaders understand that they are called to plant and water with excellence, with faithfulness, and with joy. Yet once they have planted and watered well, they trust God for the increase. This is the freedom of the steward leader. It is the freedom to understand their role, to do it passionately, and to leave the outcomes to God. When they are freed in their identity to do God's work God's way, they can follow this formula and know the joy of the steward leader.

When steward leaders look outward and engage in the relationships around them, this next step on the spiral means that they no longer see people as means to their own ends, but they are able to treat them as ends in themselves. That is, by trusting God with their identity, relying on God for the outcomes, and being secure in who they are in him, they can now invest themselves in the lives of the people around them. The agendas of others become more important, and they understand that their best work for their church or ministry will come as a result of being fully the people God created them to be. They move from managers who try to shape employees into the mold they need them to be to fellow travelers who seek to unfold their employees so that God may help them blossom into the fullness for the purpose for which he created them. They take time for relationships, they don't ask "return on investment" questions, and they are willing to suffer loss because they understand that the measurable outcome of a relationship is not what serves them, but how they can serve others.

The final step is just as easy on the upward spiral as the downward. Having proclaimed that everything belongs to God, when steward leaders look at the resources of time, the talents of others, the financial resources God gives them, and the created world, they submit them to him and seek guidance for the way he would have them invest these in his work. They resist the temptation to shift their security to what they have accumulated or their reliance on their own strength and abilities for success.

Your Next Steps

My hope in concluding with these two spirals is that you will use them to assess where you are right now in your life and leadership. Which of these spirals sounds more like your daily experience as a leader? Can you relate to any of the steps on either spiral? I believe the most important thing you can do right now is to honestly identify exactly where you are.

If you find yourself on the upward spiral, I want to encourage you today to continue this path of surrender, trust, and faithfulness that will take you further up that journey. If you are on the downward spiral, I want to shout out to you in the loudest possible voice, "Stop!" Stop right where you are. Take a careful assessment of your situation. According to the definition of these spirals, ask yourself how you got there. Look back at the beginning of your day and find out where your attitude became dominated by owner-leader thinking. Ask how it has impacted your time in the Word, your time in prayer, and your intimacy with Christ. Examine your identity, the sources of your self-worth. Where have you started listening to counterfeit voices? By identifying the fruit, you can begin to find the root of the problem. The next step is to name that root. In every place where you find yourself on this downward spiral, it's critically important that you name it. Write it down and share it with someone close to you. Confession is the first step toward walking out of a downward spiral. Pray that God would help you overcome the forces that are pushing you down this road.

I encourage you to examine your heart and attitude toward the way you see your life. Right now, at this moment, lay this book down. Open your hands up and raise them up to God and say out loud over and over again, "All that I have and all that I am is yours, Lord. The whole of my life, it all belongs to you. I surrender it back to you. Grant me, Lord, the heart of a steward."

Trust the Holy Spirit to create in you the heart of the true steward. Look out at all the things that, just moments ago, were causes of stress and fear and anxiety, and lift them back to God. Remember, your life is his, your business is his, your church is his, your ministry is his, your marriage is his, your children are his, your health is his, your future is his, your reputation is his, and your money is his—*it's all his!* And if you love him and if you trust him, this one set of statements is a beginning of your emancipation. It is the start of your road to freedom. That is the journey of the faithful steward and the life of a steward leader.

My Five Commitments
as a Steward Leader

—∞∞∞—

This final section is your place to create your battle plan. To create your plan, follow these steps for each of the three areas below.

1. Look back at the commitments you made on pages 44, 57, 63, 71, 77, and 87. Pray through them and transfer them to the five commitment sections below.
2. Go back to page 92 and consider the scriptures you recorded there. Match one key scripture to each of your five commitments. These should serve as a challenge and inspiration for each commitment.
3. Go back to page 92 and remember the allies you listed. Choose one or two allies for each of the five commitments you made, and be ready to share these commitments with them and work out a role for them to walk with you as you seek to be faithful in carrying out each one.

This will complete your battle plan. The final step is to decide how you will integrate it into your daily life. Pray diligently over this and see how God might lead you to make these commitments part of your time in prayer, devotion, self-reflection, interactions with your neighbors, and your discernment of how you will handle your time, talents, and resources.

May God bless you richly as you take these next steps in your journey of becoming a steward leader.

My Commitment to One-Kingdom Living:

_____

_____

_____

_____

Scriptures that will encourage me:

_____

_____

_____

_____

Allies who will walk beside me:

_____

_____

_____

_____

Discipline: "I will pray each day to die to the need and desire to control, step off my throne, and rise again as a free and faithful steward."

My Commitment to Intimacy With God:

_____

_____

_____

_____

Scriptures that will encourage me:

_____

_____

_____

_____

Allies who will walk beside me:

_____

_____

_____

_____

Discipline: "I will pray each day that God would reveal to me the next deeper step he is calling me to take in my relationship with him and grant me the courage and faith to take it."

My Commitment to Self-Image in Christ:

_____
_____
_____
_____

Scriptures that will encourage me:

_____
_____
_____
_____

Allies who will walk beside me:

_____
_____
_____
_____

Discipline: "I will begin each day affirming the balance God seeks in my self-image and pray not to be pulled in either direction. I will surrender my identity in my job back to God each day, refuse to play the owner, and take on the mantle of the steward of my position."

My Commitment to Presence with My Neighbor:

_____

_____

_____

_____

Scriptures that will encourage me:

_____

_____

_____

_____

Allies who will walk beside me:

_____

_____

_____

_____

Discipline: "I will begin each day with a prayer that God would enable me to see my neighbors and coworkers as he sees them. I will ask for the heart to join them on their journey and be used by God to bless, encourage, and challenge them in ways that are in line with his will for them."

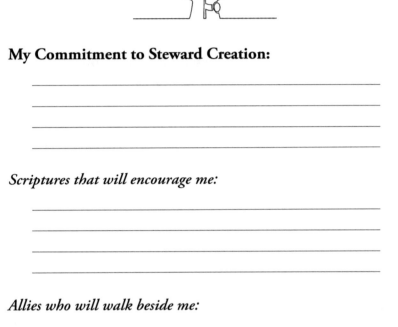

My Commitment to Steward Creation:

_____
_____
_____
_____

Scriptures that will encourage me:

_____
_____
_____
_____

Allies who will walk beside me:

_____
_____
_____
_____

Discipline: "I will begin each morning submitting my time, talents, and resources to God's work. I will pray for the heart and vision to lead a lifestyle that reflects a love and care for God's creation."

Closing Thoughts

B eyond the successful achievement of our mission and our strategic goals, God calls us as individuals and as faith communities to be witnesses in this world. We must never forget this overarching responsibility. We do not serve the kingdom of God if we meet our strategic goals, but do so in a way that bears witness to worldly values and secular measurements. If we build our success on a poor stewarding of our people's time and talents, we have failed in our call. If we claim victory in a fundraising campaign when the world sees manipulation and coercion as our tools, we have built in vain. We can become the false spiritual facades of which Jesus said, "You are like whitewashed tombs, which look beautiful on the outside but on the inside are full of dead men's bones and everything unclean" (Matthew 23:27).

How many fallen leaders fit this description? When they failed to allow the Holy Spirit to do the internal work of transforming in them the heart of the godly steward, they became the owner-leader. When they fail, their organizations pay a heavy price, but the greatest damage done is to the reputation of the kingdom of God. All the frontal attacks by atheists and Christ-haters in the media and literature combined have done less damage to the witness of the body of Christ than have a few exalted Christian leaders who have failed to live consistent lives as godly stewards.

Please hear me when I say that you cannot walk this journey alone. Isolation, self-assurance, and a lack of transparency lie at the heart of most all leadership failures. As you take this journey of becoming a steward leader, make sure you submit to the accountability of others who understand your goals and will help you see your blind spots, challenge bad assumptions, and encourage you at every step. This is a serious battle, and we cannot fight it alone. What is at stake in our Christian ministries and churches is not just missional effectiveness, but transformational witness.

What does the world see when it looks at your ministry? Not in brochures, videos, and annual reports, although they are important, but when they talk to your employees, walk your grounds, attend your events, listen to your board members, and view your work in your community with other leaders and organizations? What do they say about you when they see you at your daughter's soccer game, encounter you in a slow checkout line at the grocery store, or drive behind you on the freeway? Consistency and witness are integrally tied. If the enemy cannot make us unfaithful, he will try to make us ineffective. And we lose our effectiveness as steward leaders when we model inconsistent behavior and allow our organizations to do the same. What we lose is our witness, which means we bring shame upon the name of Jesus Christ.

This final admonition points once again to the damage that can be done by the owner-leader. If you are attempting to lead while in bondage to the need to control, you *will* fail. Your organization will falter and you will do damage to the witness of Jesus Christ in this world. Those are very high stakes! This is why throughout scripture, God consistently called men and women to leadership who loved him. They were anointed before they were appointed. They sought his face before all else. And they succeeded not because of their own abilities, but because they were God's man, God's woman. "Yahweh is looking for those whose eyes are looking back toward heaven, those with whom the Spirit can make eye contact."[16] For this reason, the first level of our created relationship is intimacy with God. And we are back to the start.

This daily intimacy arises again as the very core from which the steward leader leads. It is the beginning point on the journey of transformation. It is God's deepest desire for us. The great church father Irenaeus proclaimed that the glory of God is in man fully alive.

And so, I return to the questions I posed at the outset of this journey:

- Are you prepared to go deeper in your faith than you have ever gone before?
- Are you ready to be used by God in more powerful ways than you ever thought possible?
- Do you desire to bless the people you serve and the organizations you are called to lead?
- Are you ready for the journey?

That is your calling, your hope, and your promise. God can make you "fully alive" as a faithful steward leader who responds with joyful obedience in every area of life. We would add to Irenaeus's quote, "The glory of the kingdom of God is the leader who is completely free." Through such a leader, God can do great things for the kingdom. And chief among them is the consistent work of a community of faithful, God-honoring stewards who bear witness to the world of the transformational work of the Holy Spirit in their lives. The result of leading as a steward leader is a community *fully alive*. To God be the glory!

---

16 Korch, 57.

The Steward Leader Prayer

Lord forgive my rush to perform. It has distanced me from true intimacy with you;

Lord forgive the imbalance that I have allowed to take hold in my understanding of who I am in you;

Lord forgive my use of relationships for my own means;

Lord forgive my poor use of time and my lack of care for your wonderful creation;

Grant me a heart that daily hungers and thirsts for authentic intimacy with you;

Help me see myself as you see me and give me deep contentment with that view;

Grant me a passion to love my neighbor and a willing heart to be present with them;

Grant me the wisdom to use my time, talents, and resources to build your kingdom and the heart of a true steward of your beautiful creation.

In the name of the one who sets us free, Jesus Christ our Lord, amen.